ECUMENICAL RECEPTION

ECUMENICAL RECEPTION

Its Challenge and Opportunity

William G. Rusch

WILLIAM B. EERDMANS PUBLISHING COMPANY
GRAND RAPIDS, MICHIGAN / CAMBRIDGE, U.K.

© 2007 William G. Rusch

Published 2007 by
Wm. B. Eerdmans Publishing Co.
2140 Oak Industrial Drive N.E., Grand Rapids, Michigan 49505 /
P.O. Box 163, Cambridge CB3 9PU U.K.

Printed in the United States of America

12 11 10 09 08 07   7 6 5 4 3 2 1

Library of Congress Cataloging-in-Publication Data

Rusch, William G.
Ecumenical reception: its challenge and opportunity / William G. Rusch.
p.   cm.
ISBN 978-0-8028-4723-2 (pbk.: alk. paper)
1. Reception (Ecumenical relations)   2. Ecumenical movement.   I. Title.

BX9.5.R35R87   2007
280′.042 — dc22

2007018526

www.eerdmans.com

Pro Thora iterum
et nunc
Pro Anna quoque,
spes futurae

Contents

Preface

As a word and as an idea, *reception* has acquired an almost unprecedented use in ecumenical thought in recent decades. This development has been anything but predictable; in 1977, the German theologian Franz Wolfinger asked whether *reception* had been forgotten in the Church.[1] Yet only six years later, in 1983, the American theologian Thomas Ryan described it as "the new holy word" of the ecumenical movement.[2] What caused this dramatic shift from oblivion to notoriety? As we shall see, an ancient concept in Christian theology was being described by a new word. This new word, *reception,* was bringing a venerable idea back to center stage in a new context.[3]

Often in the history of movements, words take on special significance. This phenomenon discloses something of the character and interests of those movements. This is certainly the case for the ecumenical movement and its use of *reception.* The word enjoyed some prominence

1. Franz Wolfinger, "Die Rezeption theologischer Einsichten und ihre theologische und ökumenische Bedeutung: Von der Einsicht zur Verwirklichung," *Catholica* 37 (1997): 202-233.

2. Thomas Ryan, "Reception: Unpacking the New Holy Word," *Ecumenism* 82 (1983): 27-34.

3. For the sake of clarity, I will be italicizing *reception* in the following pages when referring to this fundamental idea.

as a technical term in the early days of the movement, subsequently waned, and then returned again to the center of attention in the 1980s. Its significance has only increased since then — in 1993 the Canadian theologian Gilles Routhier assembled a bibliography of over 250 titles devoted to the topic.[4] However, the increase in attention was not always positive; largely through overuse, a lack of clarity about the meaning of *reception* began to be obvious. What was taking place can only be understood within the larger context of the ecumenical movement, as I will demonstrate.

In 1988 I wrote a small volume on this subject, tracing the developments to that time.[5] That work made clear that significant reflection on *reception* would be needed in the ecumenical movement in the years to come. At that time I saw my work as filling a place between articles that were beginning to emerge and a major treatise that would eventually be required.

In 2006 the Lutheran World Federation, which held the world rights to both the English and German editions of my 1988 work, returned those rights to me. I am indebted to the Federation and especially to its General Secretary, Dr. Ishmael Noko, for this action.

During the years between 1988 and 2007, both reflection about *reception* and experience in attempting to engage in it have progressed rapidly. At the beginning of the new century, *reception* is proving to be far more difficult than once imagined. It may not yet be time for the definitive treatment of this subject, but it is obviously a time to reexamine it, and this is what the following pages seek to accomplish.

Chapter 1 provides some preliminary comments on *reception* and its use in various fields. Chapter 2 looks at *reception* as a Christian theological process, especially as it is found in the Bible. Chapter 3 explores "classical" *reception* in the history of the Church, from the earliest Christian centuries until the twentieth. Chapter 4 traces the history of

---

4. Gilles Routhier, *La reception d'un concile* (Paris: Éditions du Cerf, 1993), pp. 243-61.

5. William G. Rusch, *Reception: An Ecumenical Opportunity* (Philadelphia: Fortress, 1988) and *Rezeption: Eine ökumenische Chance* (Stuttgart: LWB-Report 22, 1988).

the discussion of *reception* in the twentieth century. Chapter 5 deals with the new phase of *reception,* which arose in the context of the ecumenical movement — what we might call *"ecumenical reception."* Chapter 6 turns to some examples of the ongoing process of *ecumenical reception* with its early successes and failures. Chapter 7 addresses what is needed for *ecumenical reception* to proceed in the twenty-first century. It offers the use of two new ecumenical concepts, "differentiated consensus" and "differentiated participation." Chapter 8 offers a summary and final word on the topic.

This book could not have been written without the assistance and encouragement of William B. Eerdmans Jr. and Norman A. Hjelm. I owe them a word of sincere thanks. The usual disclaimer is operative in the following pages: all errors are mine alone.

WILLIAM G. RUSCH

Chapter 1

Reception: Some Preliminary Comments

This book explores the use of *reception* as a word and as a concept. Its primary focus is on the reality and understanding of *reception* in the history and thought of the Christian Church. However, *reception* has had a remarkably rich and varied history, and has been employed in several areas of human reflection. These must at least be noted before we turn our attention to the specifically Christian context.

Wherever *reception* has been used, it has carried with it a basic meaning that can be traced back to the Latin root *cap, cep, cip.* The verb *capio* was where this root was primarily expressed, but we can also see it in *recip*, which appeared in such forms as *recipio* and *receptio.* Other Latin words similar in either derivation or meaning are *accipere* and *suscipere;* and *firmare, confirmare,* and *comprobare.* The key meaning in each of these words is "to receive," "to accept," or "to take over."

This constellation of forms and meanings made its way into English by way of Old French. The English word *reception* comes specifically from the Latin *receptio.* Its basic meaning in late Middle English, which it never lost, was "an action or fact of acquiring something." The *New Shorter Oxford English Dictionary* provides a convenient short history of the word from this point onward.[1] From the original meaning just noted, a number

---

1. *The New Shorter Oxford English Dictionary,* 5th ed., vol. 2 (Oxford: Oxford University Press, 2002), p. 2486.

of others emerge, including (but not limited to) the following: "an action of taking in, containing, or accommodating a person or thing;" "an action of learning or understanding;" "an action of receiving, especially a person or a fact;" "a formal or ceremonious welcome;" "a special occasion or a formal party;" "a place where guests or clients report on arrival at a hotel or office;" "an action of giving credit to or accepting something."

From this very brief overview it becomes clear that the word *reception* — and its correlates in other languages that draw on the Latin — is available to convey the notion of an act of "taking over" or "acquiring" something from someone else.[2] Thus *reception* has become a technical term in a number of disciplines to describe an action of "receiving" or "transfer" of knowledge or information. In all cases, this receipt or transfer carries with it certain presuppositions, including the following: at least a partial similarity between the two parties involved; language that is to some degree common; freedom on the part of the receiver to refuse what is being offered; a difference between the parties such that the content of what is received must have a certain newness; and a sufficient frame of time for the action of receipt or transfer to occur. A result of this process is a real change in both the sender and the receiver. It is more than merely an increase in knowledge; some real consequences occur for both parties. Receiver and sender should, by the acceptance or *reception,* enjoy a new relationship with one another.

Reception as a concept spent much of its history as a legal term, beginning to be used in the seventeenth century to describe a process whereby, at the end of the Middle Ages and beyond, Roman law was taken over into European and especially German law.[3] By the nineteenth century, this use was firmly ensconced in the legal scholarship, and it was not until the 1960s that *reception* began to be widely utilized in other fields.[4]

2. Thus one has in French *reception;* in German *Rezeption;* in Italian *recezione;* and in Spanish *recepción.*

3. See Dietmar Schanbacher, "Rezeption," in *Historische Wörterbuch der Philosophie* 8 (1992): 1004-8; and Frederick M. Bliss, *Understanding Reception: A Backdrop to Its Ecumenical Use* (Milwaukee: Marquette University Press, 1993), pp. 114-19.

4. See Franz Wieacker, *Privatrechtsgeschichte der Neuzeit unter Berücksichtigung der deutschen Entwicklungen,* 2d. ed. (Göttingen: Vandenhoeck & Ruprecht, 1967); and "Zum

Reception: *Some Preliminary Comments*

One such field is that of literary studies, in which *reception* has become the descriptor for a process that takes place between a text and its reader. The idea is not that a text contains a thought or some other content that a reader receives from it; rather, it is that the reader is deliberately included in the process of interpretation and analysis. The very reality of a literary composition is regarded as dependent on the comprehension of the reader, and texts are seen as having trajectories that are determined by an extended process of *reception* and reinterpretation. Thus, attention is given to what happens on the receiving side of the communication and what role the reader plays in determining the meaning of a given text. *Reception* in this context is often viewed as an existential event, implying an individual and personal decision on the part of the reader regarding the meaning of the text. Indeed, some critics have raised the question of whether a text can have any meaning whatsoever apart from its reader, and whether multiple meanings are inherent in any given text.[5] (The latter inquiry has been noted in regard to ecumenical texts, and we will consider it in that context later under an exploration of *ecumenical reception*.)[6]

Key figures in this scholarship have been Jacques Derrida, Hans-Georg Gadamer, and Hans Robert Jauss.[7] The latter can be taken as a representative example. A German who lived out his life in the twentieth century and who studied under such major figures as Gadamer and Martin Heidegger, Jauss became a leader of the so-called "Constance school" of literary criticism. In the course of his work, he developed the concept of "reception aesthetics," which referred to his contention that works of art were to be understood in terms of their receiver as much as

---

heutigen Stand der Rezeptionsforschung," in *Festschrift für Joseph Klein,* ed. Eric Fries (Göttingen: Vandenhoeck & Ruprecht, 1967), pp. 181-201.

5. See Robert C. Holub, *Reception Theory* (London: Methuen, 1984).

6. See Chapter 5, "The Emergence of *Ecumenical Reception*."

7. Representative works include Derrida's *Of Grammatology* (Baltimore: Johns Hopkins University Press, 1974); Gadamer's *Truth and Method* (New York: Continuum, 1975); and Jauss's "Rezeption, Rezeptionsästhetik," *Historisches Wörterbuch der Philosophie* 8 (1992): 996-1004. For an overview of the entire subject, see Bruce Ellis Benson, "Text Messages: Gadamer, Derrida, and How We Read," *Christian Century,* March 22, 2005: 30-32.

they were in terms of their creator; receivers, in this view, are equal co-producers of any given work's meaning. Thus *reception* is a conversation involving the producer, the work, and the receiver. And in what he called his "literary hermeneutic," which was composed of the triad of understanding, interpretation, and application, Jauss assigned priority to the receiver's aesthetic experience of the work. A key point in his thought is that the contemporary understanding of a piece of literature's meaning will be different from the original one, given in the past.[8]

Reception as understood in literary criticism has had a considerable influence in other fields of study, including classics and biblical literature, and to a somewhat lesser extent in systematic and historical theology.[9] It has found particular usefulness in the area of philosophy, where, for example, Hans Blumenberg has employed the term in connection with his study of *Epochenschwelle* ("epochal thresholds").[10] According to Blumenberg, the transition that takes place from old to new, from one epoch to another, is not to be understood as a transfer or transformation, but as *reception* in which a recasting *(Umbesetzung)* of functions of conscience and global understanding takes place.[11]

---

8. A helpful summary of Jauss's thought is given in Ormond Rush, *The Reception of Doctrine: An Appropriation of Hans Robert Jauss' Reception Aesthetics and Literary Hermeneutics,* Testi Gregoriana, Serie Teologia 19 (Rome: Editrice Pontificia Università Gregoriana, 1997), pp. 8-124.

9. For its use in biblical studies see, for example, Bernard C. Lategan and William S. Vorster, *Text and Reality: Aspects of Reference in Biblical Texts* (Philadelphia: Fortress, 1985); Edgar V. McKnight, *The Bible and the Reader: An Introduction to Literary Criticism* (Philadelphia: Fortress, 1985); and Reinhold Gregor Kratz and Thomas Krüger, eds., *Rezeption und Auslegung im Alten Testament und in seinem Umfeld* (Göttingen: Vandenhoeck & Ruprecht, 1997). For classical studies, see Ellen Greene, ed., *Re-reading Sappho: Reception and Transmission* (Berkeley: University of California Press, 1998). For historical theology, see Elizabeth A. Clark, *History, Theory, Text: Historians and the Linguistic Turn* (Cambridge, Mass.: Harvard University Press, 2005). And for systematics, see Elizabeth Schüssler Fiorenza, *Foundational Theology* (New York: Crossword, 1994).

10. Hans Blumenberg, "Epochschwelle und Rezeption," *Philosophische Rundschau* 5 (1958): 94-120.

11. Hans Blumenberg, *Die Legitimität der Neuezeit* (Frankfurt am Main: Suhrkamp, 1966).

Hans-Georg Gadamer is another philosopher who has utilized *reception,* albeit without detailed exploration of the term. But it is worth mentioning his discussion of *Horizontverschmellung* ("horizon-merging").[12] For Gadamer, reader and text enter into conversation with each other. Going into this conversation, the reader has certain understandings and prejudices; these form the reader's horizon, which is challenged by the text's horizon. In this process, a common meaning between text and reader emerges, as the two horizons come together. The elements of this process are understanding *(intelligere),* interpretation *(explicare),* and application *(applicare).*[13]

Certain parallels have been noted between the basic notion of *reception* and the concept of "inculturation." This latter term has been defined as the insertion of new values into an individual's heritage and worldview, giving it obvious similarities with *reception.*[14] Inculturation has been part of the history of the Church from biblical times, as Christianity has spread across the globe. Its emphasis on allowing all peoples to enjoy and develop their own culture and yet be authentic Christians gives it a different focus from *reception,* but there have been attempts over the years to describe inculturation in terms of *reception.*[15]

Reception, then, is a term with a rich history and a wide range of uses. It remains to be seen whether its use in some of these other fields will prove fruitful in regard to ecumenical studies. Recently the Commission on Faith and Order of the World Council of Churches took up the subject of hermeneutics, but the subject of *reception* went largely untreated in its final report, despite the hopes of some members of the

12. Discussed in *Truth and Method.*

13. See *Truth and Method,* esp. pp. 275ff.

14. See John Waliggo, "Inculturation," in *Dictionary of the Ecumenical Movement,* 2d ed., ed. N. Lossky, J. M. Bonino, J. Pobee, T. F. Stransky, G. Wainwright, and P. Webb (Geneva: WCC Publications, 2002), pp. 571-72. This article has a useful bibliography. It is also worth consulting "enculturation" and "inculturation" in the *Shorter Oxford English Dictionary,* vol. 1, pp. 822, 1351.

15. See, for example, the discussion in Frederick M. Bliss, *Understanding Reception: A Backdrop to its Ecumenical Use* (Milwaukee: Marquette University Press, 1993), pp. 125-32; and Allen Brent, *Cultural Episcopacy and Ecumenism* (Leiden: Brill, 1992).

Commission.[16] However, Ormond Rush, whose work was noted above, has suggested that the aesthetics and literary hermeneutics of Jauss could be resources to assist in the *reception* of doctrinal and ecumenical texts.[17] Likewise, literary scholar Linda Gaither emphasizes a shift in critical focus — from author and work to reader and text — that offers promise for ecumenism.[18] We will take up both Rush's and Gaither's insights later in this volume.

We turn now from this wider stage to focus on *reception* in the specifically Christian setting.

16. See *A Treasure in Earthen Vessels: An Instrument for an Ecumenical Reflection on Hermeneutics,* Faith and Order Paper 182 (Geneva: WCC Press, 1998); and P. Bouteneff and D. Heller, eds., *Interpreting Together: Essays in Hermeneutics,* Faith and Order Paper 189 (Geneva: WCC Press, 2001).

17. Rush, *The Reception of Doctrine,* esp. pp. 122-24 and 181-84.

18. Linda L. Gaither, *To Receive a Text: Literary Reception Theory as a Key to Ecumenical Reception,* American Universities Studies, Series VII, Theology and Religion 192 (New York: Peter Lang, 1997).

Chapter 2

Reception as a Christian
Theological Process

Having looked briefly at the history and manifold uses of *reception* in the last chapter, we can now turn our attention to *reception* as a Christian theological process. Our effort will be to investigate the understanding of the term in the life and thought of the Church, and to consider its effects, particularly in the area of ecumenism.

Reception in the Christian context has to be understood in terms of the revelation of the Triune God. It is the Father who sends the Son, who in turn gives the Spirit. The Spirit allows human beings to receive the good news of God's love for creation. Thus *reception* in this setting is an effect and sign of the Spirit's presence; no mere legal category, it is a theological process that is constitutive of the life of the Church.[1]

It makes sense, therefore, to begin our inquiry by looking at the Bi-

---

1. See Yves Congar, "La 'réception' comme réalité ecclésiologique," *Revue des sciences philosophiques et théologiques* 56 (1972): 500-14. Translated into English as "Reception as an Ecclesiological Reality," in *Concilium* 77, ed. G. Alberigo and A. Weiler (New York: Herder & Herder, 1972), pp. 43-68. Also see Heinrich Fries, "Rezeption: Der Beitrag der Gläubigen für die Wahrheitsfindung in den Kirchen," *Stimmen der Zeit* 1 (1991): 3-18; and Günther Gassmann, "From Reception to Unity: The Historical and Ecumenical Significance of the Concept of Reception," in *Community-Unity Communion: Essays in Honour of Mary Tanner,* ed. Colin Podmore (London: Church Publishing House, 1998), pp. 127-29.

ble, where we can delineate four different dimensions of *reception*.[2] First, the Bible itself is in part the product of *reception*. Scholars today acknowledge that the majority of biblical texts are the written deposit of earlier oral and/or written traditions. The process of selection, editing, and reshaping by which these early materials gained a written and fixed form has been designated as *reception* in the fields of form- and redaction-criticism.

Second, *reception* as a word and idea is found in the text of the Bible. In the Old Testament, we can discern the motifs of receiving and re-receiving as early as Genesis 1, in which the world receives its being from its Creator. Later, Israel as a people and a nation receives its existence by the election and covenant of God, and receives the Promised Land. Individual Israelites receive the title "servant of God." Throughout the narrative of the Hebrew Scriptures, Israel receives and re-receives God's gifts of mercy and love. In addition to Genesis 1, Exodus 19–24, Deuteronomy 7, Isaiah 34, and Jeremiah 2 are key texts for understanding this important theme.

In the New Testament — which from the Christian perspective proclaims the fulfillment of promises made in the Old — *reception* abounds. Jesus receives his mission from his heavenly Father, and he receives his place and role as a human being from the history of Israel (Matt. 1–4; Mark 1; Luke 2–4), so that the Lord of the Church receives before his Church receives from him. Likewise, the community of faith receives from Christ through his words and deeds, so that events of *reception* mark the beginning of the Christian Church. Jesus speaks in the Parable of the Sower of the word that is received (Mark 4:20), and instructs his disciples that whoever does not receive the kingdom of God like a little child will not enter it (Mark 10:15). The author of the Gospel of John recognizes the importance of *reception,* emphasizing the idea of receiving Christ as the Word: "His own received him not, but to all who received and believed was given power to become children of God" (John 1:11-12).

2. Günther Gassmann, "Rezeption I," in *Theologische Realenzyklopädie,* XXIX, 1/2 (Berlin: Walter de Gruyter, 1998), pp. 132-34.

The Book of Acts, telling the story of the early Church, continues to stress *reception:* those who receive the preaching of Peter are baptized (Acts 2:41); the followers of Jesus receive the Word (8:14, 11:1, 17:11). Acts 15 is extremely significant, giving an idealized description of an ecclesial *reception* process in which the decision of the apostolic council of Jerusalem is transmitted by messengers to the church in Antioch, and the church there rejoices at the decision.

Likewise the Pauline and deutero-Pauline corpus speaks of it. Paul recalls for the Corinthians that they have received the gospel he preached (1 Cor. 15:1) and that they have received the Holy Spirit (2:12; cf. 1 Thess. 2:13 and Col. 2:6). He informs the Christians at Rome that through Christ he has received grace and apostleship (Rom. 1:5), and reminds them that those accepted by Christ are to accept one another (15:7).

Paul also makes a clear connection between *reception* and the process of tradition. He introduces accounts of the institution of the Lord's Supper with technical rabbinic terms denoting a process of receiving tradition (1 Cor. 11:23). Several times he employs the terms *paradidomai* and *paralambanein,* the Greek equivalents to these rabbinic terms, for the process of handing on the tradition. Paul has received that which he passes on to the Corinthian Christians, which they in turn are to receive and pass on to others.[3] Tradition is understood as the process by which God gives himself to humankind — a gift that is not only a message, but a conversation between God and human beings.

There are also passages in the general epistles that refer to *reception.* The promised eternal inheritance is received (Heb. 9:15); the kingdom is received (Heb. 12:28); the gospel is received as a gift to be shared (1 Pet. 4:10).

While the study of *reception* in the Bible should not be limited to a word study, it is useful to observe that in the New Testament *reception* is expressed mainly through the two verbs *lambanein* and *dechesthai.*

---

3. For a discussion of *reception* at Corinth see Emmanuel Lane, "La reception dans l'eglise ancienne," in *La Recepción y la Comunión entre las Iglesias,* ed. H. Legrand, J. Manzanares, and A. Garcia y García (Salamanca: La Universidad Pontificia, 1997), pp. 82-88. This material also appears in English in *The Jurist* 57:1 (1997).

Lambanein and related words are used rather more explicitly for the active grasping of something given; *dechesthai* and its relatives have more varied and subjective meanings. These involve glad and reverent acceptance, inner assimilation, and practical adoption.

From this succinct overview it should be clear that *reception* is a theme that pervades the New Testament — throughout its pages, the Lord and what he gives in word and deed are of central importance.[4] This is true even where the specific terms "receive" and "accept" are not utilized. In every case, what is accepted has its own intrinsic authority. What is accepted is a new and special thing in each situation, and those who receive it are neither able to stand in judgment over it or to add to its content. All they can do is make room for it in and around themselves, with the help of the Spirit. This is the heart of *reception* in the life of early Christian congregations. While they may differ in the details, the books of the New Testament all describe a process of *reception* that is not legal and formal, but rather a glad process of receiving the Lord and the good news of his gospel through the Holy Spirit. Knowledge of the historical facts about Jesus Christ is given as well, but the Church receives above all a person, and is received in turn as the body of that person, Christ. In this biblical sense, *reception* lies at the heart of Christian faith, and the Church may be said to be the end product of the process of *reception* begun in the Bible.

Third — to return to our list of the dimensions of *reception* in the Bible — there is *reception* by the Church of the canon of Scripture.[5] "Canon" in this context denotes a standard by which certain writings are accepted or received into a collection of authoritative writings, and in doing so it implies that other books were not received because they were

4. Other instances of the use of "receive" and "accept" include Matthew 18:20, 28:20; John 14:17, 15:26, 16:13; Ephesians 5:9; 1 Timothy 3:15; 1 John 5:6.

5. A detailed account of the development of the canon lies outside the scope of this work, but it can be pursued at great length in the following titles: H. von Campenhausen, *The Formation of the Christian Bible* (Philadelphia: Westminster, 1972); Bruce M. Metzger, *The Canon of the New Testament* (Oxford: Clarendon, 1987); and B. S. Childs, *Biblical Theology of the Old and New Testaments: Theological Reflections on the Christian Bible* (Minneapolis: Fortress, 1993).

deemed non-authoritative. The word "canon" employed in this manner goes back to the fourth century of the Christian era (which is when the New Testament reached its present form), but the idea of a collection of authoritative texts is much older than that. The earliest churches claimed the Hebrew Scriptures as their own because they believed that they alone had the correct understanding and interpretation of those books. Yet at almost the same time, these churches were beginning to add to this canon writings that told the story of the Christ-event and preserved the preaching, teaching, and life of these original communities.

In this process of addition, the question arose quite early as to which writings were to be regarded as authentic witnesses to this history. The debate became particularly acrimonious in the second century, with the reductionism of Marcion at one end of the spectrum and the expansiveness of the Gnostics and Montanists at the other.[6] The books that were finally received underwent very different processes: some, like the Gospels of Matthew, Mark, Luke, and John, quickly secured universal acceptance. Others had a more difficult time of it: the Book of Revelation, for instance, was initially accepted in the East, then rejected, then accepted by the whole Church after a long, painful process of debate. In the end, two standards came to be applied: whether the writing in question was used for reading in the worship of the Church; and whether the writing was considered to be derived from an apostle or someone writing with an apostle's authority. Such developments make it clear that the canon evolved slowly and by a process of *reception*.

Fourth, there is *reception* as a Christian theological practice that takes place ever anew within the Church as the biblical message is interpreted and proclaimed. Such disciplines as historical criticism, form criticism, and redaction criticism are all tools of *reception,* and current debates about the authority of Scripture can be viewed as struggles over *reception.* The seriousness of *reception* is demonstrated by the fact that

---

6 Marcion would have limited the canon to the Gospel of Luke and some selections from the Pauline corpus; the Gnostics and Montanists would have increased the size of the canon to include books conveying their special teachings.

such struggles have the capacity not only to unite churches, but to divide them as well.[7]

From this exploration of *reception* as a Christian theological practice, we can discern several important facts. First, *reception* has a place in Christian reflection and practice quite apart from any of its legal, literary, and philosophical roles, on which we touched briefly in the last chapter. And long before systematic thought was given to *reception* in Christian circles, it was practiced. Indeed, we could make the case that the Christian Church could not have arisen or continued to exist throughout some twenty centuries without active engagement with *reception.* Implicit in the practice of *reception* was a view of the Church as a community of local congregations in fellowship with each other and with gifts to share. It involved an understanding of the Christian faith as something to be handed down from generation to generation. And it was essentially personal, something that at its deepest takes place in Eucharistic communities and includes all members of those communities. Further, *reception* is a continuing process, for the Church can only exist throughout time as it receives the *kerygma,* the gospel of the Christ-event. This means that there must be an appreciation of *reception* as a spiritual event of transmission and acceptance, and that theory and practice must be united. In fact, at all times in the history of Christianity, the practice of *reception* has preceded reflection about it.[8] Thus *reception* is a basic characteristic of Christian faith and life, reflecting the process of *reception* that proceeds within the Triune Godhead.[9]

7. Examples could be given from the current debates within the Episcopal Church, the Evangelical Lutheran Church in America, and the Presbyterian Church (U.S.A.) about human sexuality and the literature that these churches have produced on this subject. Behind these discussions lies the question of the *reception* or non-*reception* of certain views of authority and its locus. See J. Neil Alexander, *This Far by Grace* (Cambridge, Mass.: Cowley, 2003); and Karl Paul Donfried, *Who Owns the Bible? Toward the Recovery of a Christian Hermeneutic* (New York: Crossroad, 2006).

8. Gilles Routhier, *La reception d'un concile* (Paris: Éditions du Cerf, 1993), pp. 181-242.

9. For a description of this patristic insight, see Eugene F. Rogers Jr., *After the Spirit: A Constructive Pneumatology from Resources Outside the Modern West* (Grand Rapids, Mich.: William B. Eerdmans, 2005), pp. 144-48.

However, in this lively process in the Church there is much more than simply a slavish acceptance of what has gone before. Certainly the Word of Jesus and the apostolic proclamation of the Christ-event are the constant base. Yet there is always an element of interpretation called for in changed and new situations. Evidence of this interplay between constant base and new situations can already be seen in the New Testament itself, as challenges face the second and third generations of Christian believers (see 1 Tim. 2:7 and 2 Tim. 1:11); and what is begun in the New Testament continues onward throughout the history of the Church.[10]

Therefore it is appropriate now to look at this process of *reception* in the history of the Church prior to the twentieth century.

---

10. See Hermann Brandt, ed., *Kirchliches Lehren in ökumenischer Verpflichtung: Eine Studie zur Rezeption ökumenischer Dokumente* (Stuttgart: Calwer Verlag, 1986), pp. 95-97.

Chapter 3

A History of *Reception* from the Early Church until the Twentieth Century

In the last chapter we saw how *reception* has been an intrinsic and integral component of Christian faith and life — indeed, how without it the Christian Church would be an impossibility. It is now fitting to move to an examination of how *reception,* again as a word and as an idea, has functioned in the history of the Church up to the twentieth century.

As we proceed, a terminological shift is in order. In this chapter and the next, we will see how the twentieth century has a claim to be a new chapter in the history of Christian *reception.* We will therefore designate *reception* prior to the rise of the modern ecumenical movement in the early twentieth century *classical reception,* and we will call *reception* as a phenomenon within the ecumenical movement *ecumenical reception.*

Classical Reception and the Early Church

In the earliest years of the Church's existence, there was not a formalized process of *reception.*[1] Nevertheless it was an ongoing, informal

---

1. For another description of *reception* in the early Church, see Frederick M. Bliss, *Understanding Reception: A Backdrop to Its Ecumenical Use* (Milwaukee: Marquette University Press, 1993), pp. 66-67; and Klaus Schatz, "Die Rezeption ökumenischer

process that had its impact on the faith, life, and unity of the growing Church. Its locus was the local church, with its members and the increasingly clear profile of officeholders such as elders and deacons. In the first two centuries, *reception* was involved in two particular processes: the securing and handing on of the Christian faith with its ecclesial life and structures; and the protection and consolidation of the fellowship and unity of local churches. In both these areas *reception* was regarded as a work of the Holy Spirit.

Over time, *reception* could be seen in the formation and broad acceptance of confessional formulae and liturgical texts among the churches, practices that would lead to the development of the creedal statements of the fourth century and later. *Reception* led to the development and acceptance of a specific structure of officeholders in the local churches — a trajectory whose development was encouraged by concerns to protect the faith against false alternatives. *Reception* among local churches called forth and led to the realization of local and regional councils or synods, gatherings of which took place in Egypt, North Africa, Gaul, and Corinth in the course of the second and third centuries. These meetings would provide a model for the ecumenical councils of the fourth century onward. Throughout this time, *reception* was a defining feature of the development of the canon of Scripture, which we discussed in the last chapter.

A glance at some of the writings from this period will illustrate how *reception* played out in certain settings. To the Apostolic Fathers *reception* is connected with a kind of intellectual and spiritual acceptance that is much less personal than in the New Testament and that is a matter of consolidating what has already been given. In the text known as *First Clement*, probably originating in Rome in the last years of the first century, the writer speaks of receiving "our symbol" (58.2). And Ignatius of Antioch, in his *To the Magnesians*, speaks of being confirmed in the ordi-

---

Konzilien im ersten Jahrtausend — Schwierigkeiten, Formen der Bewältigung und verweigerte Rezeption" in *Glaube als Zustimmung: Zur Interpretation kirchlicher Rezeptionsvorgänge*, Quaestiones Disputatae 131, ed. W. Beinart (Freiburg: Herder, 1991), pp. 93-119.

nances of the Lord and his apostles (13.1), a concept he gleans from such New Testament passages as Hebrews 13:9 and Colossians 2:7.

In the second century, Irenaeus of Lyons and Origen stand as examples of Church Fathers who engaged the idea of *reception*. Irenaeus employs the concept in his famous *Adversus haereses* in order to refute those who have departed from the true faith. And in his *De Principiis,* Origen notes the importance of the apostles' receiving and handing on to believers the words and teachings of Christ.

In all these early references to the faith being handed down, we need to remember that a significant component of *reception* was oral; literacy was not widespread as it is today.[2] Nevertheless, local churches did exchange letters among one another; it was by this means that Christians were received from one local church to another, elections of bishops were shared and received, and decisions of local synods were communicated. Such letters, too, served as a critical means of informal *reception* of church life and teaching.[3]

The primary understanding of *reception* in the Church's first three centuries, though, had to do with the process by which local and regional councils or synods were made known and accepted by other local churches.[4] These gatherings were most often concerned with settling disputes, such as that over the date of Easter, and with refuting such heresies as Gnosticism and Montanism.[5] Undergirding such councils was the presupposition that any particular local church was authentically the Church only as it lived in communion and fellowship with other local

2. See Bliss, *Understanding Reception,* pp. 43-52.

3. See Bliss, *Understanding Reception,* pp. 67-68; and P. Nautin, *Lettres et Ecrivains chrétiens des IIe and IIIe siècles* (Paris: Éditions du Cerf, 1961).

4. In this period the words "synod" and "council" can be used interchangeably. Both refer to a local assembly of bishops to discuss and to decide matters of importance to the faith and life of the local (diocesan) churches. The retention of both words in the following description is a reminder of how these early local meetings became the forerunners of the "ecumenical" councils of the fourth century and later.

5. For more on these synods and their agendas, see É. Junod, "Naissance de la practique synodale et unité de l'Église au IIe siècle," *Revue d'Historie et de Philosophie religieuse* 68 (1988): 163-80; and A. Fischer, "Die Synoden im Osterfeststreit des 2. Jahrhundert," *Annuarium Historiae Conciliorum* 8 (1976): 15-39.

churches; according to the belief and teaching of the Church at this time, each council or synod, irrespective of its size, had the Holy Spirit, with its authority based on the known and recognized orthodoxy of its participants and its ability to call forth *reception* from the church. Each church, then, potentially had the ability to speak for the whole Church. Here again we see the importance of the role of the Holy Spirit in *reception*.[6]

There is still research to be done in order to truly understand the precise steps by which any given council or synod came to be regarded as ecumenical in the early Church. Nevertheless, we can highlight several characteristics. First of all, when what is to be received already exists in a vital way in the original sources of faith of the receiving community, the process of *reception* is quicker and easier. Familiar ideas do not present the problems of strange suggestions. Second, the process is not cut-and-dried; it can be more or less complicated, depending on what is being received.[7] Finally, in all instances of *reception* there is an understanding that what is being accomplished is not merely a juridical action of acceptance on the part of church officials. Rather, the juridical action is understood as the beginning of a spiritual process by which the entire community reaffirms its commonality with the earliest Christian communities and with other churches.

Another important element in the early development of *reception* that cannot be overlooked is the evolving theology of the episcopacy. Local bishops were coming to be seen not only as the heads of their individual congregations, but also as the voice of their local church in relationship to other local churches. Thus there was a kind of natural system for resolving issues that arose, and bishops assembled in councils with increasing frequency. The pattern was clearly political, and built on the model of the Roman Senate. Often when a given matter was brought to

6. In an important article on *reception,* Aloys Grillmeier pays attention to these local gatherings: "Konzil und Rezeption," *Theologie und Philosophie* 45 (1970): 331-37.

7. Grillmeier traces out this process for the Council of Chalcedon in the Roman Catholic Church. Admittedly Chalcedon is not a local council for most of the churches of the East and West, but the article makes apparent the numerous steps that were involved. "The Reception of Chalcedon in the Roman Catholic Church," *Ecumenical Review* 22 (1970): 383-411.

resolution, the members of the synod would compose a conciliar letter that would be sent to the churches.

Beginning in the year 190, councils convened in Italy, Gaul, and Corinth to address issues related to a proper understanding of the Eucharist.[8] Soon after, such councils were also being called in Egypt, North Africa, and Asia Minor. By the time of Cyprian, in the middle of the third century, regional synods or councils, usually comprising the bishops of a Roman province, were regularly convoked at the major city of the area. Cyprian viewed the synod as the expression of the unity of the episcopate, a unity based on the thought that all bishops possessed the one Seat of Peter, so that each local church was fully apostolic and the Church. The notion that each bishop had to express his unity with other bishops by taking part in a council or synod was a step toward the idea of a larger council, one beyond local dimensions. The execution of that idea was still some years in the future, but it would come.

Some councils, naturally, were more significant than others — a salient example is that of the Synod of Antioch, which met in the year 268. This local synod condemned one Paul of Samosata, Bishop of Antioch, for using the term *homoousios* to describe the relation of the Son to the Father. When the Council of Nicea some fifty-seven years later employed the very term *homoousios* in its confession of faith about the relation of the Son to the Father, the residual authority of the Synod of Antioch was so great that the members of the Council of Nicea felt a need to defend the decision of the Synod of Antioch, despite their own use of the term.[9] Here is a vivid illustration of *reception* of a local council's decision by the entire Church, a *reception* so powerful that it cannot be ignored.

In all these ante-Nicene synods, the role of formal juridical acts seems relatively minor. Seen as a whole, *reception* is conceived as a spiritual and theological process of confirmation and completion. Even if

8. Eusebius, the first historian of the Church, is a major source for information about such synods or councils; see especially his *Ecclesiastical History* V:24-25, 34.

9. Athanasius did this by insisting that the term had to be seen in its historical context. See his *De synodis* 3. On the question of Paul of Samosata's use of *homoousios*, see G. W. H. Lampe, in H. Cunliffe-Jones and B. Drewery, eds., *A History of Christian Doctrine* (Philadelphia: Fortress Press, 1978), p. 88.

there is a certain narrowness compared with the breadth of *reception* found in the New Testament, it is the wider framework of a spiritual event of transmission and acceptance that provides the key to understanding *reception* as it operated in local and regional synods prior to 325.

But as with so many things in the early Church, Constantine forms a dividing line.[10] Regardless of Constantine's original intentions, the effects of his intervention in church affairs were profound.[11] Councils were no longer concerned only with the preservation of sacramental communion in the Church, but were now involved in decisions about questions of faith that affected the peace and security of the Roman Empire as a whole. And their decisions were no longer merely shared by synodical letter for approval by churches, but were accepted directly by the emperor and given the status of imperial law. In theory, the councils did have a certain amount of freedom, but the deep involvement of the emperor in the conciliar process resulted in a certain amount of obligation and cooperation with him. In this context *reception* developed a new and critical meaning: that is, whether and to what extent a council in its acts was being obedient to the truth of the faith. From the fourth century on, *reception* of any council's work was a theological and spiritual process of decision in the life of the Church, a process in which laity, religious, and clergy participated to a striking degree — and with an enthusiasm that would seem strange to many people today!

The Council of Nicea of 325 provides a good example of this new kind of *reception*. Its decisions were received only after some fifty-six years of quarrels and disputes, punctuated by synods, excommunications, exiles, imperial interventions, and violence. Synods in Tyre and Jerusalem ten years later rehabilitated Arius, whose views had been con-

10. See Bernard Sesboüé, "La Réception des Conciles, de Nicee a Constantinople II et Ses Ensignements," in *La Recepción y la Comunion entre las Iglesias,* ed. H. Legrand, J. Manzanares, and A. García y García (Salamanca: Universidad Pontificia, 1997), pp. 121-57.

11. See John Zizioulas, "Development of Conciliar Structures in the Time of the First Ecumenical Council," *Councils and the Ecumenical Movement,* World Council of Churches Studies 5 (Geneva: WCC, 1968), pp. 48-49.

demned as heresy at Nicea, and deposed Athanasius, champion of the Nicene interpretation of the faith. Even the Bishop of Rome, Pope Julius, did not seem certain that the decisions of Nicea were irrevocable.

By contrast, the Council of Ephesus of 431 met in circumstances that did not help its claim to be ecumenical. Cyril of Alexandria rushed through a decision before the arrival of bishops from Syria, and only later agreements between Cyril and his followers and John of Antioch gave Ephesus some right to be called ecumenical. This council gives an example of non-*reception* in that it was the major cause for the creation of the "Nestorian church" and a schism that would endure for over a thousand years.

These examples should make clear the evolution of *reception* in the years after Constantine; they are typical of the councils of the day, some of which met with quick *reception* (such as the Third Council of Constantinople in 681), some with complicated processes of *reception* (such as the Council of Chalcedon in 451 and the Second Council of Constantinople in 553), and some with what amounted to non-*reception* (such as the Armenian and Coptic responses to the Council of Chalcedon). Fluctuation in the relationship between East and West, the evolving role of the papacy, political rivalry, and questionable interpretations of texts all came to influence the process.[12]

Hermann Josef Sieben has highlighted the consistence of the ideas of *consensio antiquitatis* and *consensio universitatis* in the *reception* of the councils of the period from 325 to 787.[13] These ideas made such councils a risky business, for they had to document a consensus of the entire Church at a moment in history (the *consensio universitatis*) that was demonstrably consistent with Scripture and its proclamation (the *consensio*

---

12. For presentations of these councils that go beyond the scope of this volume, see Sesboüé, "La Réception des Conciles," pp. 142-53; Christopher M. Bellito, *The General Councils* (New York: Paulist, 2002), esp. pp. 27-33; and Norman P. Tanner, S.J., ed., *Decrees of the Ecumenical Councils*, vol. 1 (London: Sheed & Ward, 1990), esp. pp. 1-156.

13. Hermann Josef Sieben, *Die Konzilidee der Alten Kirche*, Konzilen-Geschichte, Series B, Untersuchungen (Paderborn: Schöningh, 1979), pp. 511-16; see also Edward J. Kilmartin's summary "Reception in History," in *The Search for Visible Unity*, ed. Jeffrey Gros (Cleveland: Pilgrim, 1984), pp. 48-50.

antiquitatis). As we have seen, neither of these was always an easy task. The success of any council was determined not so much by the formal juridical authority it could claim, but rather on how successful it was in establishing these two kinds of consensus. Of the two, there is some evidence that *antiquitatis* enjoyed some priority over *universitatis.*

We can make a number of other observations about *reception* in the patristic church after Nicea. It was sometimes surprising and unexpected; it could not be programmed. It often had dimensions of hermeneutics or interpretation: churches after receiving a council were free to propose new documents to be received, and so a process of *reception* and re-*reception* could occur. It could not be commanded. It could be postponed, but postponement was not to be identified with rejection.

Reception in the patristic church was taking place in areas besides that of councils and synods as well. Among the most notable was that of liturgy. As the great liturgical traditions of the Eastern and Western churches were established, extensive exchange of liturgical practices and texts occurred. This exchange was facilitated by the view that all local churches held the same faith and so had gifts to share with one another, and the openness of the churches to one another made the process of *reception* easy, particularly compared to that of the councils.

Among the many possible examples is the widespread *reception* of the epiclesis, that part of the Communion liturgy that invokes the Holy Spirit, in the divine liturgy of the East during the fourth century. Both the influence of controversies over the divinity of the Third Person of the Trinity, and probably the epiclesis of Hippolytus' *Apostolic Tradition,* played a role. There is no doubt that the *reception* of the epiclesis was a major factor in the development of the Eastern theology of the Eucharist.

A number of liturgical feasts spread through the Church and were received. Marian feasts such as the Purification, the Nativity, and the Presentation gradually spread from East to West, and local canonizations of saints took place in the West until the thirteenth century. This practice was viewed as liturgical rather than juridical, and by means of *reception* between churches, a local cult would be established and extended. Not all such exchanges were positive, of course; sometimes local practices were lost and liturgies distorted by alteration. But at least in the early centuries dangers were recognized and the *reception* of different liturgical practices was accompanied by an insistence on the freedom of the local church to determine its own liturgical practices.[14] This attitude was reflected with regard to laws and customs as well: there were both a toleration of and a will toward *reception*.

On the other hand, there is certainly evidence of some non-*reception* with respect to liturgy and church life as well. The Trullan Synod of 692 issued some 102 canons, but Pope Sergius, who was not a Westerner by birth, refused to accept them in the West, apparently because in his view they had little direct relationship to church life there. Conversely, the Council of Sardica, which met from 343 to 344, promulgated a canon stating that problems between churches should be referred to the Bishop of Rome, whose decision should be accepted as final. Not surprisingly, this canon was never received in the Eastern church.[15]

As this survey of the early Church discloses, long before systematic thought was given to *reception, classical reception* was practiced. The Church in this early period simply lived out *reception*. Implicit in this practice was a view of the Church as a community or fellowship of local churches with gifts to share with each other. There was an understanding of the Christian faith as something to be handed down from generation to generation and as something essentially both personal and communal. The focal point for this *reception* was the local church, and it included the proclamation of the gospel, a canon of Scripture, a ministry in apostolic succession, and an exchange of letters and decisions of synods. There was an awareness that *reception* is a spiritual process that takes place in Eucharistic communities, and in fact makes Eucharistic sharing a reality. The ultimate standard for this sharing is the gospel itself, transmitted since the apostles, which involves all members of the

14. Both Ambrose of Milan (*De sacramentis* 3.1.5) and Gregory the Great (*Epistle* 1.43) show an appreciation for local variation.

15. See Edward J. Kilmartin, "Reception in History: An Ecclesiological Phenomenon and Its Significance," *Journal of Ecumenical Studies* 21 (1984): 34-54.

communities and is an ongoing process. Hence *reception* was fundamental to the life of the Church and for individual Christians, occurring
under the guidance of the Holy Spirit.

Classical Reception in the Medieval Church

The coming of the Middle Ages in the West brought a new context in
which several characteristics of *classical reception* as practiced in the
early Church ceased to exist.[16] For example, a new ecclesiology appeared in the West that did not see the Church as a fellowship or community of local churches bound together but rather saw the Church as a
universal corporation in which clergy and laity expressed their opinions
on important issues. When an agreement was reached on matters of
doctrine and discipline by the appropriate representatives (and on the
highest level this would be the pope), this was to be regarded as the inspiration of the Spirit and the consensus of the faithful. The responsibility of all was to accept the decision, and no other form of *reception*
was believed to be needed.[17]

    Reception, therefore, came to be viewed as a part of constitutional
law. A sharp distinction was made between teaching and learning in the
Church, with one part of the Church considered active and the other
passive. With the development of such an ecclesiology, *reception* as
practiced in the patristic church became impossible. Adolf Lumpe has
shown how in this period the acceptance of papal decretals in the courts
and schools of canon law was designated *reception.* This process developed a tradition reaching back to the dictum of Gratian, claiming support from both Augustine of Hippo and Isidore of Seville. Lumpe

16. For additional descriptions of the medieval Church see Bliss, *Understanding Re-
ception,* pp. 87-97; and Klaus Schatz, "Die Rezeption ökumenischer Konzilien im ersten
Jahrtausen — Scwierigheiten, Formen der Bewältigung und verweigerte Rezeption," in
Glaube als Zustimmung, ed. Beinart, pp. 119-21.

17. See Kilmartin, "Reception in History," pp. 35-36; and Johannes Muhlsteiger,
"Rezeption — Inkulturation — Selbst — Bestimmung," *Zeitschrift für katholische Theologie* 105 (1983): 268.

points out this usage by Pope Honorius III in his bull *Liber sextus*.[18] In the *Codex iuris canonici* and the attached *Professio catholicae,* the word *recipere* appears often in the sense, "to recognize," "to approve," or "to sanction."[19] Although this vocabulary can be traced back to the fifth century and the writings of Pope Gelasius I, especially to his *De recipiendis et non recipiendis,* it is apparent that much of the original richness of the concept of *reception* had been lost.

As the Western church grew more hierarchical in nature, *reception* receded more and more into legal categories.[20] This development did not occur in the East, where at least in theory a vital link was always maintained between *reception* and the active participation of all the faithful. Even in the West authors like Hincmar of Rheims could as late as the ninth century maintain an ecclesiology that recognized the Church as a fellowship or community, and saw ecumenical councils as called by the emperor and made up of numerous bishops who played an active role in *reception*.[21] But the tendencies that led to Pope Honorius III had already been established. Pope Damasus and the synod of 368 had maintained that the ecumenicity of a council required papal approval, and this view was repeated by Leo the Great and by Gelasius I. Until the sixteenth century, the Western church became increasingly papal and *reception* more and more a matter of canon law.

The fifteenth century supplies unambiguous evidence of non-*reception*. It is well known that the original text of the Nicene-Constantinopolitan Creed did not contain the Latin word *filioque,* "and the Son," immediately after the phrase "the Holy Spirit who proceeds from the Father." The insertion of the word into the creed by a Western church gradually spread and soon after the year 1000 was adopted at

18. Adolf Lumpe, "Zu 'recipere' also 'gultig annehmen, anerkennin' im Sprachgebrauch des römanischen und kanonischen Rechts," *Annuarium Historiae Conciliorum* 7 (1975): 129-30.

19. Lumpe, "Zu 'recipere'," pp. 130-31.

20. For a summary of the place of *reception* in canon law see Gilles Routhier, *La reception d'un concile* (Paris: Éditions du Cerf, 1993), pp. 37-40.

21. Hincmar, *Opusculum LV,* Capit c. 20.

Rome. But this insertion was never accepted in the East, and since the time of Photius in the ninth century it has been an issue of disagreement between East and West. The Council of Florence, meeting from 1438 to 1445, endeavored to secure a reunion between the Greek church and the church of Rome. Under political pressure and as part of a scheme for re-union, the Greeks accepted the teaching of the *filioque* but not its addition to the Creed. The plan, however, was short-lived. The compromise at the Council of Florence was never accepted in the East. A number of Orthodox synods refused to ratify the union between the Latins and Greeks. Although regarded by the Roman Catholic Church as the six-teenth or seventeenth ecumenical council, the Council of Florence was never successful in making this claim in the East and in having its teach-ing accepted there. Thus in a large segment of the Church a council with broad representation and papal approval could not even under diverse formulations substantiate its claim to be faithful to the *consensio antiquitatis*.[22]

Classical Reception in the Churches of the Reformation

The sixteenth-century Reformation in the Western church was at least in part a reaction against the ever-increasing papal domination of the Church and claims that the papacy was the final and highest authority in the interpretation of Scripture. It amounted to a call for a return to the apostolic norm of the gospel, which according to the Lutheran and Cal-vinist Reformers had been clearly identified by the writers of the patris-tic church. In the heated debates of the early decades of the sixteenth century, the Reformers appealed to the need for a general council inde-pendent of and free from all papal control. Although the various Re-formers were not in total agreement about the nature of such a council, it was clear that what was intended was a council that would have au-thority to the extent that its decisions were in accord with the witness of Scripture. Thus there was a standard for the *reception* of church deci-

22. See Bellito, *The General Councils*, pp. 91-93.

sions as well as an understanding of councils as having no absolute infallibility — something the Reformers believed they saw adequately demonstrated by the endless series of councils in the history of the Church. Yet ecclesial *reception* was not a matter of indifference to the Reformation; in the history of the Reformation churches, processes of *reception* are conspicuous.

Article 1 of the Augsburg Confession reveals a *reception* of the Nicene Creed by the Lutheran Reformers: "In the first place, it is with one accord taught and held, following the decree of the Council of Nicea . . ."[23] Article 3 indicates the *reception* of the Apostles' Creed by the same Lutheran Reformers.[24] A bit further along, Article 7 is concerned with the Church. In speaking about what is required for true unity, reference is made to the importance of agreement about the teaching of the gospel and the administration of the sacraments. Such consensus must be based on the *reception* under the Spirit of certain teachings by all the community.[25]

The Calvinists as well as the Lutherans expressed a desire to identify with the creeds of the early church. Parallels to Articles 1 and 3 of the Augsbug Confession can be found in the *Confessio Helvetica Posterior* of the Reformed tradition, and the Apostles' Creed is explicitly adopted in the Heidelberg Catechism.

The Reformers accepted the need to receive and to interpret earlier doctrinal decisions of the Church; in time, they extended these needs to their own confessions. The validity of Lutheran and Reformed confessions, then, was not based upon approval of a church magisterium, but

23. This is the most recent and widely used English translation, from *The Book of Concord,* ed. Robert Kolb and Timothy Wengert (Minneapolis: Fortress, 2000). The original German and Latin can be found in *Die Bekenntnisschriften der evangelish-lutherischen Kirche* (Göttingen: Vandenhoeck & Ruprecht, 1959).

24. *Book of Concord,* pp. 38-39.

25. *Book of Concord,* pp. 42-43. Here the Latin is clearer than the German: ". . . satis est consentire de doctrina evangelii et de administratione sacramentorum," as opposed to ". . . dies ist gnug zu wahrer Einigkeit der christichen Kirchen, dass da einträchtiglich nach reinem Verstand das Evangelium gepredigt und die Sakrament dem gottlichen Wort gemass gereicht werden."

rather on their claim to be faithful witnesses to and interpreters of Scripture. Over the years, they were no longer seen as merely the writings of individuals; rather, the churches of the Reformation assumed a responsibility for them.

In the case of the *Book of Concord* of 1580, the claim was made not only that the Lutheran churches were speaking, but that the one, holy, catholic, and apostolic Church could find its teaching in these confessions. The complete title of the *Book of Concord* illustrates the status of these confessions and the importance that was attached to their *reception* within the churches: *Concordia: Christian, Reiterated, and Unanimous Confession of the Doctrine and Faith of the undersigned Electors, Princes, and Estates who Embrace the Augsburg Confession and of their Theologians, Together with an Appended Declaration, Firmly Founded on the Word of God as the Only Norm, of Several Articles about which Disputation and Strife Arose after the blessed Death of Martin Luther, Prepared for Publication by the Unanimous Agreement and Order of the aforementioned Electors, Princes, and Estates for the Instruction and Admonition of their Lands, Churches, Schools, and Descendants.*[26] These same ideas can be found at the conclusion of the first part of the Formula of Concord, in which the signers declare that they are describing not only their own faith but that of all pious Christians who stand with the Word of God, the three creeds, and the earlier Lutheran confessions.[27] We can see, therefore, that *consensio antiquitatis* and *consensio universitatis*, which were so important to the early church, were not matters of indifference to the Reformers, who claimed that their teaching, in distinction to that of Rome's, did have antiquity and universality. As Luther put it, "I hold, together with the universal Church, the one universal teaching of Christ, who is our only master."[28]

Also like the early church, the churches of the Reformation found that their documents did not always meet with immediate acceptance.

---

26. *Book of Concord*, p. 1.

27. *Book of Concord*, pp. 524-31.

28. Martin Luther, *Sincere Admonition to All Christians*, in *Luther's Works*, vol. 45, ed. Walter I. Brandt (Philadelphia: Muhlenberg, 1962), pp. 70-71.

Indeed, the process of *reception* continued for some time after the formulation of the confessions in the sixteenth century. While it is true that no further documents were accorded confessional status, the number of officially recognized confessions varies in the different churches of the Reformation. Even within Lutheran churches today this is true, as many give greater weight to the Augsburg Confession and to Luther's Small Catechism than they do to other documents. An excellent review of the process of the *reception* of the Augsburg Confession has been provided by Wolf-Dieter Hauschild.[29] Tracing its vicissitudes from its creation in 1530 through the twentieth century, he demonstrates that the route the Confession took to its preeminent status among Lutherans was much more complex than we might think. One thing that becomes clear is that different interpretations of the Confession continually modify the sense in which it claims authority.[30]

Of course, *reception* in the sixteenth century, just like its counterpart in the patristic church, should not be seen as limited to theological documents. Even the confessions must be viewed in the context of a larger, ongoing process of *reception* that began with the Reformation and continued beyond it, facing both the constants of the Christian faith and new situations. Many aspects of this process of *reception* were informal, but they were real nevertheless. Forms of piety and church life, structures of ecclesial organization, the use of new hymns and devotional writings — all of these had to undergo processes of receiving and accepting, some of which continue to the present day, affecting the relations of those churches with one another and with the Roman Catholic Church.

In theory, *reception* of new theological statements should always be

29. Wolf-Dieter Hauschild, "Das Selbstverstandnis der Confessio Augustana und ihre kirchliche Relevanz im deutschen Protestantismus," in *Evangelium-Sakramente-Amt und die Einheit der Kirche,* ed. Karl Lehmann and Edmund Schlink (Freiburg: Herder & Herder, 1982), pp. 133-63.

30. This is a point that has also been made by Ulrich Kühn, who demonstrates how the Confession must be viewed as both a subject and an object in the Church's process of tradition. See "The Future of a Tradition," in *Confessio Augustana, 1530-1980,* ed. Vilmos Vajta (Geneva: Lutheran World Federation, 1980), pp. 61-79.

a possibility for the Protestant churches. Practically, however, such *re-ception* has seldom, if ever, occurred since the sixteenth century. Two possible examples of preliminary *reception* could be the Barmen Declaration of 1934 and the Leuenberg Agreement of 1973. But views concerning the authority of the former vary widely, and the latter has been seen as applying primarily to the European situation. And so we move on from our study of *reception* in the Protestant Reformation, to consider it in the Roman Catholic context.

Classical Reception in the Roman Catholic Church

The Council of Trent met from 1545 until 1563, assembling in response to the challenges raised by the Protestant Reformation. Its decisions were certainly not received by Protestants — and even the Catholic response seemed underwhelming at first. It would be 120 years before Trent, with its clearly formulated doctrinal systems, was finally received by all the Catholics in Europe.

Earlier in this chapter we noted the tendency within the Western church to gravitate toward a monarchical view of the Church, in which the pope essentially holds the role of king or emperor. Such an ecclesiology eliminates any real need for a broad base of *reception* among the laity and even among the church hierarchy. This tendency reached its apex in the papacy of Pius IX and the First Vatican Council, which met from 1869 until 1870. Among the results of this council was the definition of papal primacy and infallibility.

Yet even here we can see signs of broader *reception*. The outbreak of the Franco-Prussian War led to the council being suspended on October 20, 1870, and in view of Pius IX's own understanding of the papal office and the decisions made by the council — especially *Pastor aeternus,* which defined the infallibility of the Roman pontiff — we might think that there would be little need for, or little attention given to, *reception* of the First Vatican Council's conclusions. After all, the definition implies its own *reception.* Yet a minority at the council opposed *Pastor aeternus,* and after the council was disbanded, this minority continued for a while to argue against the council's decision. In the course of time, though, they came to accept it, and many as individuals sought to explain later why they had not approved the definition at the council but ultimately were able to do so.[31] Thus we see *reception* taking place by a minority after the council. Of course, this involved a process; Johannes Beumer refers to the pastoral letter of August 18, 1870, sent by the German bishops to their dioceses urging support of the council's decisions as one important element in this process.[32]

All this reveals that even in the post-First Vatican Roman Catholic Church, with its high view of the papacy, earlier understandings of *reception* were not totally lost. A valid council does not depend just on the pope, no matter how powerful the pope may be. Somehow, the larger church is involved. Theologians would go on to debate whether a broader *reception* only brings to explicit validation what was already present in the council's decision or whether the validation was in some way necessary, with the argument tending toward the conclusion that a broad *reception* cannot alter the inner being of a conciliar decree, and that non-*reception* cannot in and of itself be taken as a sign of false teaching; it may merely mean that the proposed decree is inopportune.[33] But never was the idea seriously expressed that broad *reception* could be eliminated from the life of the Church. Practically speaking, its role may have been minimized since 1870.[34] Yet it has lived on as an idea with a long history, and was in fact brought to discussion by the Second Vatican Council, whose *Lumen gentium* described a process of *reception* in which all the faithful of the people of God exercise specific charisms for the renewal and building-up of the Church. *Reception,* therefore, should not be dismissed too quickly as not functioning in the Roman Catholic Church of today.[35]

31. See Johannes Beumer, S.J., "Das Erste Vatikanum und seine Rezeption," *Münchner Theologische Zeitschrift* 27 (1976): 261.

32. Beumer, "Das Erste Vatikanum," pp. 264-68.

33. Beumer, "Das Erste Vatikanum," pp. 270-72.

34. See H. J. Pottmeyer, *Towards a Papacy in Communion: Perspectives from Vatican Councils I and II* (New York: Crossroad, 1998), esp. pp. 74-109.

35. *Lumen gentium* 12 and 13.

A *History of* Reception

Classical Reception in the Orthodox Church

In contrast to the West, where it tended to be viewed as something of a legal term, *reception* in the East retained an integral role in the broader faith and life of the Church. Orthodox theology developed no unified explanation of the nature and role of *reception,* but certainly we can identify certain themes. *Reception* involves agreement with the faith of the Church as the final authority in matters of belief. It is the fruit of the charismatic work of the Spirit, and as such cannot be brought under official control. The Orthodox churches see in *reception* a dialectic between laity and clergy, both of whom have a critical role under the inspiration of the Holy Spirit.

Such views created a tension in Orthodox thought between, on the one hand, the position that an ecumenical synod or council is the highest authority, and, on the other, the position that a council's decisions can only be considered valid when they are accepted by the whole Church. In the last century, the theologian Nikolaj Afanassiev, building on the work of Aleksej Chomjakov, taught that decisions of councils are dependent on *reception* by the faithful. But not all Orthodox theologians accepted this conclusion, and debate on the subject continues.[36]

Yet there is agreement within Orthodoxy that *reception* is, in the final analysis, spontaneous. It is not organized by juridical forms or directives. This is not to say that it is a plebiscite, but rather that it has its origin in the action of the Holy Spirit, who dwells in the Church, supports it, and maintains it in the true faith. For Orthodox theologians, the Church is complete only as the body of the faithful. Only in this totality, with this support of the Spirit, is the Church capable of infallibility; an ecumenical council is only a delegation from the body of the faithful, and only to the extent that it is faithful to the Church as a totality can it make the claim to be ecumenical. According to Orthodox thinking, a council is an organ whose infallibility results from, and is an expression

36. Waclaw Hryniewicz, "Die ekklesiale Rezeption in der Sicht der orthodoxen Theologie," *Theologie und Glaube* 65 (1975): 260-63.

of, the infallibility of the Church.[37] For the Orthodox, *reception* of conciliar decisions, books of Scripture, and so forth, is possible only to the degree that what is received is seen as a truthful expression of the tradition of the gospel. *Reception* under the Holy Spirit's inspiration has a prophetic character; it is a recognition of the gospel itself. It is a proclamation of the Episcopal leadership of the truth in the context of the active support of the faithful of the Church. These characteristics reflect an understanding of *reception* that can be traced far back in Christian history, as we have seen, and that can certainly make a contribution to the understanding and practice of *reception* in an ecumenical age.

From this all too brief overview of *reception* prior to the rise of the modern ecumenical movement in the early twentieth century, several insights can be gleaned. *Classical reception* was never merely the acceptance of theological texts from church councils or synods; it was never merely a juridical process. Rather, it has always functioned as an ongoing process, which in a real sense can be said to have predated the institution of the Church and to be led by the Holy Spirit. It involves the constant practice of interpretation and reinterpretation as new circumstances and situations present themselves. It is not repristination; it is the lively process of the Church drawing on the resources of its past to seize and accept the present activities of the hovering Holy Spirit. Always it includes the willingness of local churches to receive from other churches. Clearly, then, to ask the churches of today to engage in the same kind of *reception* is to ask them to do nothing less than involve themselves in a process that is at the heart of their very existence.

We turn now to the subject of *reception* in the twentieth century and especially in the setting of the ecumenical movement that came to define that period in the Church's history.

37. These ideas are developed further by Liviu Stan in "Concerning the Church's Acceptance of the Decisions of Ecumenical Synods," in *Councils and the Ecumenical Movement,* World Council of Churches Studies 5 (Geneva: WCC, 1968), pp. 68-75.

Chapter 4

A History of *Reception* in the Twentieth Century

From the previous two chapters we can see that *reception* has been a critical concept, both theoretically and practically, in the Christian faith and the life of the Church. At the beginning of the twentieth century, however, it lay largely forgotten and ignored; certainly it was practiced to some extent, but it was not a topic that made its way into theological discourse. Yet by the century's end, theologian Jean-Marie Tillard would describe *reception* as one of the most important theological rediscoveries of the twentieth century.[1] What transpired over the course of these years in regard to *reception?*

To understand *reception* in the last hundred years, we need to examine two forces that have left an indelible mark on Christianity: the ecumenical movement and the Second Vatican Council.

The history of the Church in the twentieth century can be viewed largely through the lens of the ecumenical movement, a movement — or, more accurately, a collection of movements — whose goal has been the visible unity of divided Christian churches. There were certainly attempts prior to the twentieth century to heal the splits in the Church — between East and West, and Protestant and Roman Catholic. But such

---

1. Jean-Marie Tillard, "Reception: A Time to Beware of False Steps," *Ecumenical Trends* 14 (1985): 145-48.

efforts were usually isolated; it was only in the twentieth century that divided churches entered into an ongoing and sustained movement to unite Christians and their churches.

It all began with the World Missionary Conference that met in 1910. Christian denominations and missionary societies from around the world sent 1200 delegates to Edinburgh to discuss, among many other things, how by working together they might more effectively spread the gospel. The next few decades saw a flurry of ecumenical activities, including the encyclical of the church of Constantinople in 1920, an invitation to all churches to form a league of churches, a World Conference on Life and Work held in Stockholm in 1925, and two years later the First World Conference on Faith and Order at Lausanne, Switzerland.[2]

By 1933 plans were being laid to establish a worldwide organization devoted expressly to ecumenism. These efforts continued through the difficult years of World War II, so that finally in 1948 the World Council of Churches came into being, uniting the work of the Conferences on Life and Work, and Faith and Order. Thirteen years later the International Missionary Council was integrated into the World Council. After its first assembly in Amsterdam in 1948, the council met at intervals of approximately seven years. By 1968 and the fourth assembly, at Uppsala, the World Council found itself preoccupied with the important issues of a rapidly changing and politically divided world. Considerable emphasis was placed on the economic and social development of nations in Africa, Asia, and South America, and as a result some individuals and churches began to wonder whether the council's theological commitments were being lost to social concerns.

But other events in the 1960s kept the theological aspects of the ecumenical movement in the fore. At the third assembly of the WCC, in New Delhi in 1961, four Orthodox churches — those of Romania, Poland, Bulgaria, and the Patriarchate of Moscow — joined the Council. Their presence, along with that of the Patriarchate of Constantinople (a

---

2. See Ruth Rouse and Stephen Charles Neill, eds., *A History of the Ecumenical Movement, 1517-1948,* 2d ed. (Philadelphia: Westminster, 1967), esp. pp. 405-41, 535-42, and 697-724.

founding member of the Council), helped to ensure that a balance would be struck between the equally important theological and social concerns in the work of the Council. The 1960s also saw the entry of the Roman Catholic Church into this ecumenical movement, with Pope John XXIII's creation in 1960 of the Secretariat for Promoting Christian Unity. Regular contact thus began between the Roman Catholic Church and other churches, with openness to ecumenism culminating during and after the Second Vatican Council.

In fact, it is in the calling of the Second Vatican Council in 1961 that we can find the first motivation for a renewed and contemporary attraction to *reception*. Vatican II raised serious questions — and not just for the Roman Catholic Church — about the conciliar nature of the Church, the teaching authority of the Church, and how conciliar and other teachings were to be received into and made part of the life of the Church. How did the early Church receive the decisions of the great ecumenical councils? Could the answer to this question contribute to the unity of divided churches? In questions like these, *reception* returned to the modern theological agenda after decades of neglect. Interest in *reception* was linked closely to the idea of conciliarity, with the notion of Christians gathering under the guidance of the Holy Spirit for prayer, counsel, and decision on matters affecting the Church's faith and life.

The theological effects of the Second Vatican Council were immediate and easy to document. Indeed, works began to appear even before the council began meeting in 1962 that directly or indirectly raised the topic of *reception*. *Die ökumenischen Konzile,* edited by Hans J. Margull, appeared first in Europe in 1961 and was followed five years later by an American edition.[3] The book is a collection of essays on the nature and authority of church councils by recognized scholars from the Anglican, Lutheran, Old Catholic, Orthodox, Reformed, and Roman Catholic churches. Prefaces to both the American and German editions made clear that the book was a direct response to questions raised by the call-

---

3. Hans J. Margull, ed., *Die ökumenischen Konzile* (Stuttgart: Evangelisches Verlagswerk, 1961). American edition, *The Councils of the Church* (Philadelphia: Fortress, 1966).

ing of the Second Vatican Council and by the lack of ecumenical discussion about ecumenical councils.[4] While it is true that no essay in the volume deals exclusively with *reception,* the subject is touched upon repeatedly. Georg Kretschmar, in his discussion of the councils of the ancient churches, notes without further elaboration the need for Spirit-wrought *reception* of conciliar decisions.[5] Later in the same piece he points out that *reception* is a constantly new task for all Christians, having as its norm the apostolic word.[6] Christians must, Kretschmar argues, constantly discern which of the ancient councils faithfully reproduced the apostolic word. In another essay, Edmund Schlink observes that *reception* has undergone many transformations in history. He notes that early churches recognized that a council can err, and that their *reception,* therefore, was an important confirmation of what a given council had decided. There should be a parallel, he contends, between the early Church and the member churches of the WCC, in that resolutions should be received by the churches rather than simply proclaimed by representatives at an assembly.[7] And Emilianos, Orthodox Bishop of Meloa, stresses the role in Orthodox thought of the Spirit in *reception,* as well as the important place of both bishops and laity in the *reception* of ecumenical councils of the Orthodox.[8]

The discussion in this book makes it clear that *reception* was becoming a topic on the agenda of ecumenical conversation — perhaps not a main topic yet, but certainly one linked to many important ideas. In the same year that the German edition was published, the assembly of the WCC met in New Delhi, where again the influence of the recently summoned (but not yet meeting) Second Vatican Council was felt. The assembly requested that a study of synods and councils of the ancient church be undertaken, and the action was approved because the WCC saw the life of contemporary churches to be shaped by the great decisions of the early centuries and because the assembly believed that his-

---

4. Margull, *Councils of the Church,* pp. v, ix.
5. Margull, *Councils of the Church,* p. 23.
6. Margull, *Councils of the Church,* pp. 80-81.
7. Margull, *Councils of the Church,* p. 489.
8. Margull, *Councils of the Church,* pp. 338-69.

torical consideration of the early period, accompanied by theological reflection, might uncover the root of problems dividing the modern
churches. The Commission on Faith and Order undertook this work at
meetings in 1963 and 1964. A special group met over the next two years,
and a final report was published in 1968 under the title *Councils and the
Ecumenical Movement.*[9]

The commission's final report, "The Importance of the Conciliar
Process in the Ancient Church for the Ecumenical Movement," concen-
trates, as its title indicates, on conciliarity — that is, the fact that the
Church in all times needs assemblies to represent it — and the relationship of councils to the unity of the Church. It examines the patterns of
councils and then turns to their authority and impact, taking up the question of *reception.*[10] It defines *reception* as the process by which local
churches accept the decision of a council and thereby recognize its authority. *Reception,* therefore, is not something added to the inner authority of a council, but rather is something that confirms that council's authority. A complex, open process that can occur in many different ways,
reception is spiritual at its core and has as its norm the ancient apostolic
tradition. Its proof is precisely the long process of critical appropriation
that both precedes formal *reception* and follows it. The report concludes
by offering some comments on how conciliarity as a concept can aid the
churches to move toward a true ecumenical council in the future.

One essay in the volume, "Reception: Prolegomena to a Systematic
Study," by Werner Küppers, directly addresses *reception.*[11] Not surprisingly, Küppers places the entire discussion in the context of councils,
examining *reception* as a theological problem concerning how a given
council acquires or fails to acquire recognition and authority. He traces
a line of development from the *reception* of the conciliar process by various local synods to the great ecumenical councils with their deep involvement of the Roman emperor, perceiving its importance for reach-

9. *Councils and the Ecumenical Movement,* World Council of Churches Studies 5
(Geneva: WCC, 1968).

10. *Councils and the Ecumenical Movement,* pp. 15-17.

11. *Councils and the Ecumenical Movement,* pp. 76-98.

ing consensus on fundamental questions about Christology and the Trinity. Finally, he turns to *reception* as it relates to church division and the new *oikumene*. He recognizes the need to make room for a new *reception* process in the new conciliar life of the churches. The new *oikumene* can only be the fruit of a new conciliar life and a new process of *reception* that brings together the self-attesting truth of God and church statements that come from the *synodos* (or "coming together about this"). Acknowledging and complying with this, he contends, will constitute decisive tasks in the struggle for Christian unity.[12] Thus the earliest attention to *reception* by the World Council of Churches was intimately connected with councils, endeavoring to understand the role they might play in the Church seeking unity in the twentieth century.

This same council was also inspiring Roman Catholic scholars to give increased consideration to *reception*. In 1970 the veteran patristic authority Aloys Grillmeier wrote on the topic of councils and *reception*. In his article, "Konzil und Rezeption," Grillmeier stresses that as theologians, ecumenists, and churches take up the topic of *reception,* they need to be aware of the research done in Germany in the field of jurisprudence, where *reception* was seen as a centuries-long process whereby the legal system of the Roman Empire was received into the German legal system.[13] Accepting the conclusion of legal historian Franz Wieacker that *reception* cannot exist unless two distinct cultural areas are involved, Grillmeier argues that genuine *reception* was exogenous, not endogenous; epidemic, not endemic.[14] One takes over a law from the other. But where Wieacker traced out his legal *reception* as a process taking centuries and entailing the intellectual rationalization of the whole of public life, Grillmeier turns to *reception* as a theological concept, observing its importance to canonists and considering examples of genuine and spurious *reception* in the early churches.

In this survey, Grillmeier identifies a new and critical point: *reception*

---

12. *Councils and the Ecumenical Movement,* p. 98.

13. Aloys Grillmeier, "Konzil und Rezeption," *Theologie und Philosophie* 45 (1970): 331-37.

14. Franz Wieacker, *Privatrechtsgeschichte der Neuzeit unter besondere Berücksichtigung der deutschen Entwicklung,* 2d ed. (Göttingen: Vandenhoeck & Ruprecht, 1967).

can become a central theme of ecumenical practice and theology. It can be not merely an acceptance of texts and decisions, but a living power of critical dialogue that should lead to unity in particular and include Antioch, Alexandria, Constantinople, Wittenberg, Geneva, and Rome.[15]

In the course of his article, Grillmeier discusses the various sorts of councils in the early church, showing how they relate to different understandings of the Church. He offers the First Vatican Council as an example of a council of hierarchy, in which *reception,* at least on the part of the laity, consists merely of passive obedience. Here we can see the influence of Wieacker's exogenous *reception:* the second partner receives from the first something it did not create. Grillmeier contrasts this with the Second Vatican Council, which he sees as a model of ecumenical promise, involving as it does theologians, church leaders, and the faithful. Thus a new interpretation of *reception* as a living process rather than as a simple exchange can be expected by the churches.

In remarkable ways, Grillmeier's article was ahead of its time, identifying aspects of *reception* that would become topics of debate some fifteen years later. He expertly demonstrates the decline of *reception* in the later church, a trajectory that can be seen in the First Vatican Council. He also stresses the exogenous character of the exchange that takes place in *reception,* a point for which he is indebted to the methodological experience of legal historians. For Grillmeier, this genuine *reception* is a receiving from outside a community. It is not a simplistic model of giving, but rather a multilayered process. When one church receives from another in genuine *reception,* it is taking to itself and its life something that it has not produced: "Hence it is to be assumed that there is genuine *reception* in the ecclesial arena only where two partners are genuinely different and separated from each other and thus can enter into the relationship of giving and receiving."[16] Yet this is a view that would soon be regarded as too narrow.

---

15. Grillmeier, "Konzil und Rezeption," pp. 336-37.

16. Grillmeier, "Konzil und Rezeption," p. 331. The German text reads, "Von daher ist zu vermuten, dass es echte Rezeption im kirchlichen Bereich nur dort gibt, wo zwei Partner echt voneinder verschieden oder geschieden sind und so in das Verhältnis von Geben und Empfangen treten können."

In 1972, Yves Congar, the French Roman Catholic ecumenist, published an extremely important essay addressing many of the same topics as Grillmeier.[17] Although Congar acknowledges his debt to Grillmeier and thus to Wieacker, he finds the view of exogenous *reception* to be too restrictive, and concludes that in some instances what Grillmeier had judged to be exogenous is actually not. *Reception* between churches, after all, cannot be fully exogenous, since individual churches exist within the framework of the one Church. Congar also notes the new interest in *reception* in ecumenical circles, but he cautions that church history contains an array of different kinds of *reception* and theories about *reception*. He perceives in the Second Vatican Council a continuing interest in *reception* that can be traced back to the Councils of Nicea and Constantinople, and to other councils of the early Church in the West in the second millennium. Offering a historical review of patristic texts, he indicates how the councils of individual or local churches came, by *reception,* to be viewed as great councils of the entire Church. *Reception* of any council's conclusions, he argues, depended finally on whether the council was seen as transmitting the faith of the apostles.

Congar gives additional examples of *reception* and non-*reception,* many of which we have already considered: the acceptance of the canon and spread of liturgical forms in the former category, and the Council of Chalcedon and the *filioque* clause in the Nicene Creed of 381. He sees these processes of *reception* and non-*reception* as part of the nature of the life of the Church in history.

In one section on theological interpretation, Congar, like Grillmeier, argues that the concept of *reception* must be freed from its associations with constitutional law. It should be aligned instead with an ecclesiology that sees the whole body of the Church structured locally as individual churches and enlivened by the Holy Spirit. Underlying this ecclesiology are two conditions: first, that the universal Church cannot

---

17. Yves Congar, "La 'réception' comme réalité ecclésiologique," *Revue des sciences philosophique et théologique* 56 (1972): 500-14. The English translation of this influential text is "Reception as an Ecclesiological Reality," in *Election and Consensus in the Church,* ed. G. Alberigo and A. Weiler (New York: Herder & Herder, 1972), pp. 43-68.

err in faith; and second, that consensus is an effect of the Holy Spirit and a sign of the Spirit's presence. Congar insists that *reception* does not confer validity, but rather affirms, acknowledges, and attests that the matter undergoing *reception* is good for the Church. On the whole, his treatment is not as directly connected to the immediate ecumenical situation as Grillmeier's, but his careful historical review furnished a significant resource for an advance in the discussion of *reception*. Further, in the course of his own work on the topic, Congar offered a definition of *reception* that has often been repeated in the literature on the topic: "By 'reception' we intend the process by means of which a church (body) truly takes over as its own a resolution that it did not originate in regard to its self, and acknowledges the measure it promulgates as a rule applicable to its own life."[18]

The main ideas of both the Grillmeier and Congar articles found a forum for lively discussion when the World Council's Commission on Faith and Order met in Louvain in 1971, a year after the Grillmeier essay and a year before the publication of Congar's conclusions. At this meeting, Roman Catholic theologians took part for the first time as full members — one of the fruits of the Second Vatican Council. As both study reports presented to the commission and the documents with the reports from the meeting make clear, *reception* was entering the ecumenical vocabulary in a decisive way.[19]

The Commission on Faith and Order also explored *reception* in the context of councils — particularly in connection with the Council of Chalcedon. The Commission saw churches in the ecumenical movement to be in the process of the continuing *reception* or *re-reception* of councils, a process which raised questions about the acceptance or rejection of Chalcedon in the various traditions, about the present status of anathemas pronounced by the councils, and about various under-

18. Congar, "Reception as an Ecclesiological Reality," p. 45. The original French reads, "Par 'réception' nous entendons ici le process par lequel un corps ecclesial fait sienne en vérité une determination qu'il ne s'est pas donnée à lui-même, en reconnaissant, dans la measure promulguée, une règle qui convient à sa vie."

19. *Faith and Order: Louvain, 1971,* Faith and Order Paper 59 (Geneva: WCC, 1971), pp. 23-32 and 224-29.

standings of tradition. The "Study of the Council of Chalcedon" and "Conciliarity and the Future of the Ecumenical Movement" were to remain on the Commission's agenda, ensuring that *reception* would continue to receive attention.

Thus we can see how the Second Vatican Council moved *reception* to the center of attention, especially in the ecumenical movement, and served as a catalyst for continuing historical and theological study of the word and concept, especially as it pertained to councils of the Church.

Vatican II was not, however, merely an event that called back *reception* for theological reflection. It was also the source of a number of significant documents requiring *reception* within the Roman Catholic Church. In this sense, we can consider the Roman Catholic Church a contemporary case study of the process of *reception*. As it has come to see itself as more collegial and to view *reception* as more than a juridical decision, more attention has been given to how conciliar documents are received within that church. It is recognized that *reception* is a process that goes on after a council finishes its work; in nearly half a century since its formal close, *reception* of the Second Vatican Council's conclusions has been neither smooth nor uniform in the Roman Catholic Church. It certainly has not been completed. The process of *reception* or non-*reception* will no doubt continue for many years.

On the twentieth anniversary of Vatican II, an extraordinary synod took stock of the developments since the council. This event prompted literature that examined the *reception* that the council encountered.[20] In the years since, the topic has continued to engage scholarly attention.[21] Scholarship in the 1990s built on this earlier work and endeavored to an-

---

20. See, e.g., G. Alberigo, J. P. Jossua, and K. A. Komonchak, eds., *The Reception of Vatican II* (Washigton: Catholic University Press, 1987); and also W. Beinert, "Die Rezeption und ihre Bedeutung für Leben und Lehre der Kirche," in *Glaube als Zustimmung: Zur Interpretation kirchlicher Rezeptionsvorgänge,* ed. Wolfgang Beinert (Freiburg: Herder & Herder, 1992), pp. 15-49.

21. See Gilles Routhier, *La reception d'un concile* (Paris: Cerf, 1993), esp. the bibliography, pp. 249-51; and Routhier, "La réception dans le débat théologique actual," in *La Recepción y la Comunión entre las Iglesias,* ed. H. Legrand, H. Manzanares, and A. García y García (Salamanca: Universidad Pontificia, 1997).

alyze the constitutive elements, determinative factors, and key players in the process of *reception*.[22] Some of this scholarship has concluded that insufficient attention has been give to the topic, with emphasis instead being placed on practical application of the council in the life of the Roman Catholic Church.[23] Indeed, the fact that the word *reception* is employed only four times in the new code of canon law within the Roman Catholic Church suggests that *reception* as an ecclesiologically critical reality has not yet entered into its purview — this in spite of the fact that the new code does acknowledge a role for the laity of the church that is more than merely passive obedience. Some authorities on canon law see this failure to acknowledge *reception* as evidence of inadequate *reception* of Vatican II.[24]

These developments and perspectives are important for our purposes here if for no other reason than the fact that internal Roman Catholic attention to *reception* has had an impact on the ecumenical movement. The ultimate *reception* or non-*reception* of the Second Vatican Council's teachings will greatly influence the Roman Catholic Church's future relations to the ecumenical movement. This is true in large part because the *reception* of Vatican II will commit the Roman Catholic Church in all expressions of its faith and life to concepts that are conducive to ecumenical advance, such as an understanding of the Church as *communion,* a view of the laity as more than the passive and obedient receivers of the Church's teaching, an increased appreciation of the collegiality of all bishops, and a sense of religious liberty in the world.[25]

Vatican II authorized bilateral dialogues between the Roman Cath-

22. Routhier, "La réception dans le débat théologique actual," pp. 34-37.

23. See, for example, Ormond Rush, *Still Interpreting Vatican II: Some Hermeneutical Principles* (New York: Paulist, 2004).

24. See Peter Krämer, "Respuesta a la Conferencia de C.R.M. Redaelli," in *La Recepción y la Comunión,* ed. Legrand et al., pp. 351-53; and Eugenio Corecco, "Aspects of the Reception of Vatican II in the Code of Canon Law," in *The Reception of Vatican II,* ed. Alberigo et al., pp. 249-96.

25. See W. Beinart, "Die Subjecte der kichlichen Rezeption," in *La Recepción y la Comunión,* ed. Legrand et al., pp. 410-12.

olic Church and other churches, and due to that church's resources and size, since the 1960s multilateral work like that found in Faith and Order has been eclipsed by bilateral dialogues between churches. These conversations have had purposes ranging from promoting mutual understanding to achieving full fellowship.[26] And they have had an influence beyond dialogues directly involving the Roman Catholic Church. The dialogues that Roman Catholics have had with Anglicans and Lutherans as well as with the Orthodox and Reformed traditions have in turn had their effects on the dialogues that these churches have conducted among themselves. The past forty-five years or so have witnessed both an increase in dialogues and a demonstrable interrelation between them.[27]

The upsurge that began in the 1960s has continued without any significant abatement to the present. Since the 1970s there have been Anglican-Lutheran dialogues, Anglican-Orthodox dialogues, Anglican–Roman Catholic dialogues, Baptist-Reformed dialogues, Lutheran–Roman Catholic dialogues, Methodist–Roman Catholic dialogues, and Reformed–Roman Catholic dialogues — and this is by no means an exhaustive list. As we might expect, the reports of these dialogues have varied; nevertheless, a common motif runs through most of them: with ever-increasing stress and urgency, the reports ask the churches who sponsored them to take some action on their recommendations, hopefully to receive the results of the dialogues and to be changed by them. In short, the dialogues are asking the churches to be engaged in what is now commonly understood to be *ecumenical reception*.

---

26. See Nils Ehrenström and Günther Gassmann, *Confessions in Dialogue*, 3d ed., Faith and Order Paper 74 (Geneva: WCC, 1975), p. 10; and Warren A. Quanbeck, *Search for Understanding: Lutheran Conversations with Reformed, Anglican, and Roman Catholic Churches* (Minneapolis: Augsburg, 1972).

27. Three important English-language volumes illustrate both these points clearly: Ehrenström and Gassmann, *Confessions in Dialogue;* Harding Meyer and Lukas Vischer, *Growth in Agreement: Reports and Agreements of Ecumenical Conversations on a World Level* (New York: Paulist, 1984); and Jeffrey Gros, F.S.C., Harding Meyer, and William G. Rusch, eds., *Growth in Agreement II: Reports and Agreed Statements of Ecumenical Conversations on a World Level* (Geneva: WCC, 2000).

To give one example, in 1971 in the report of a dialogue between Methodists and Roman Catholics, often referred to as the Denver Report, there is a reference to "getting across our agreements to the Churches at large." The word *reception* does not appear, but the intention is clear. At this early stage, this dialogue is urging the sponsoring churches to take seriously what we are calling *ecumenical reception*.[28]

Official dialogue between Anglicans and Roman Catholics began in 1970 with the founding of the Anglican–Roman Catholic International Commission (ARCIC). During the first phase of its work, which lasted until 1981, it explored such issues as the Eucharist, ordination, and authority. Along the way it engaged its sponsoring churches in the tasks of evaluating its work, examining its claimed agreements, and exploring their implications; various Anglican churches and the Roman Catholic Church in its dioceses and at the Vatican prepared responses to elements of the dialogue. In response to these, the commission issued various "elucidations" to take into account reactions to its conclusions.[29] By 1977 the need for a larger evaluation of its work was recognized in the Common Declaration of Pope Paul VI and Archbishop of Canterbury Donald Coggan.[30] Five years later the Roman Catholic Congregation for the Doctrine of the Faith issued a rather negative document of observations on the report of the dialogue.[31] Nevertheless, all these efforts must be seen as early attempts to enter into the process of *ecumenical reception*. These attempts, both Anglican and Roman Catholic, reveal that both churches were entering new territory.[32]

The situation in those years was similar with regard to the dialogue between Lutherans and Roman Catholics. This dialogue, too, issued reports urging its conclusions upon its sponsoring churches. Its first report, the so-called Malta Report of 1972, called upon Lutherans and Catholics to enter into a "special life process" together. The 1978 report

28. See Meyer and Vischer, *Growth in Agreement*, §5, p. 328.
29. Meyer and Vischer, *Growth in Agreement*, pp. 62-129.
30. See Meyer and Vischer, *Growth in Agreement*, p. 127.
31. "Observations on the ARCIC Final Report," *Origins* 11 (1982): 752-56.
32. We will explore this territory further in Chapter 6.

entitled *The Eucharist* actually entitles its concluding section "Reception," noting that a theological teaching remains a theory as long as it is not affirmed and adopted by the whole people of God. It asks its churches, therefore, to examine, improve, and make their own the work of the dialogue.[33] The document on ministry of 1981 suggests that the only way to solve the issue of ministry is through a process in which the churches "reciprocally accept each other" — a process, again, that we would call *ecumenical reception*.[34] The next document from this dialogue, *Facing Unity,* asks the churches to examine, perhaps correct and supplement, and finally give authority to the dialogue's conclusions.[35] And the dialogue's latest report, 1993's *Church and Justification,* poses the question whether the several reports of the dialogue over the years do not constitute the sufficient consensus that would enable the churches to embark on concrete steps toward visible unity.[36] Again, although the word is not used, this is clearly an example of *ecumenical reception.* And although more concrete steps are needed, it should be noted that the Lutheran World Federation has in fact asked its member churches for reactions to the dialogue.[37]

Further examples could be given. As early as 1981 the dialogue between the Roman Catholic Church and the Disciples of Christ led to requests to enter into *reception*.[38] In 1983, in its fifth report, the Joint Working Group between the Roman Catholic Church and the World Council of Churches described the ecumenical situation at the time by noting that churches were being challenged to find the right way to receive the real convergences in the theological understanding of Faith and Order. And beginning in the 1970s and continuing into the 1980s,

---

33. Meyer and Vischer, *Growth in Agreement,* p. 212.

34. Meyer and Vischer, *Growth in Agreement,* p. 273.

35. See Gros, Meyer, and Rusch, *Growth in Agreement II,* p. 444.

36. See Gros, Meyer, and Rusch, *Growth in Agreement II,* pp. 486-87.

37. For an evaluation of attempts at *ecumenical reception* in Germany, see Harald Goertz, *Dialog und Rezeption: Die Rezeption evangelisch-lutherisch / Dialogdokumente in der VELKD und der römische-katholische Kirche* (Hanover: Lutherisches Verlagshaus, 2002).

38. Meyer and Vischer, *Growth in Agreement,* pp. 165-66.

the work of various dialogues resulted in meetings and consultations devoted to *reception* as a theme.[39]

In these same years, the Faith and Order Commission of the World Council of Churches began to sponsor a forum to exchange information with various Christian world communions on bilateral and multilateral discussions and to study the implications of these dialogues for the whole ecumenical movement. The first forum, held in 1978, dealt chiefly with concepts of unity, but spoke briefly to the topic of *reception*. In a subsection entitled "The Process of Reception of the Results of the Dialogues," the forum declared that *reception* is the responsibility of the churches and that the publication of dialogues' work is an intentional part of the process of *reception*. The forum also suggested that a process of several stages needs to be developed and that in the future new methodologies and the use of a broader range of expertise and analyses will be needed.[40] These comments, modest as they may be, are evidence all the same that requests for the *reception* of the dialogues' work were being heard.

The second forum, a year later, did not take up the subject of *reception* directly, but the resulting report *How Does the Church Teach Authoritatively Today?* from the Commission on Faith and Order did.[41] This report acknowledged the need for a stronger emphasis on the *reception* of teachings by the whole Church. To the degree that teachings have been arrived at by the involvement of all the faithful, *reception* is facilitated. *Reception,* according to the report, is not to be understood as just involving decisions arranged from above that are submitted to the

39. One such was a symposium held by the World Lutheran Federation, at which papers by George Lindbeck of Yale University and Lukas Vischer of the Faith and Order Commission addressed directly the topic of *reception*. See Lindbeck's "Reception and Method: Reflection on the Ecumenical Role of the Lutheran World Federation" and Vischer's "Reception and Method in Interconfessional Dialogue," in *Ecumenical Methodology,* ed. Peder Højen (Geneva: WCC, 1980).

40. *The Three Reports of the Forum on Bilateral Conversations,* Faith and Order Paper 107 (Geneva: WCC, 1980).

41. *How Does the Church Teach Authoritatively Today?* Faith and Order Paper 91 (Geneva: WCC, 1979).

community for passive *reception,* involving nothing more than endorsement. Rather, *reception* is a profound appropriation, through gradual testings, by which teachings are made a part of the life and liturgy of the community.[42]

The forum of 1980 devoted a major portion of its work to *reception,* suggesting a significant increase of interest in the topic over the course of just two years.[43] The report indicated the various meanings of *reception* and the forms it can take, as well as the belief that it ultimately occurs as Christ graciously accomplishes it by his Spirit. *Reception* was acknowledged to be more than an intellectual exercise — to be a spiritual process of communication within the Church that is both dynamic and dialogical, and that brings with it new understandings. *Reception* of joint statements, the report stated, is not an end in itself, but rather a step on the way toward fuller visible unity, a unity marked by commitment rather than simply consent.[44]

Also in 1980 the meeting of the Societas Oecumenica had as its theme "Theological Consensus and Ecclesial Reception." These conferences of the Societas were published in 1981. Even a glance at the table of contents of the volume discloses that many of the papers by ecumenists such as M. Garijo Guembe, P. Lengsfeld, H. Meyer, and M. Seils took up directly the *reception* of the results of ecumenical conversations.

One of the clearest pieces of evidence of a shift in the discussion of *reception* from councils to dialogues occurred not with a bilateral conversation but with a multilateral one. In 1982, the Commission on Faith and Order of the World Council of Churches published the document *Baptism, Eucharist and Ministry.*[45] This text was produced after some fifty-five years of work. Heavily indebted to the bilateral dialogues, *Baptism, Eucharist and Ministry* claims an ecumenical convergence on three

42. *How Does the Church Teach Authoritatively Today?* p. 88.

43. See Daniel F. Martensen, "LWF Ecumenical Relations in Review: 1980," *Lutheran World Federation Documentation* 7 (1981): 10-14.

44. P. Lengsfeld and H. Stobbe, eds., *Theologischer Konsens und Kirchenspaltung* (Stuttgart: Kolhammer, 1981).

45. *Baptism, Eucharist and Ministry,* Faith and Order Paper III (Geneva: WCC, 1982).

crucial ecumenical subjects. More than one hundred theologians from a great variety of traditions considered this text to have reached a stage of sufficient maturity that they transmitted it to their churches asking them to take up the question of *reception* and to make an official response at their highest level of authority.[46]

Continuing interest in the *reception* of *Baptism, Eucharist and Ministry* can be noted in a number of events that occurred after its publication. For example, a conference on its *reception* was held in October of 1982 in Hyde Park, Illinois; this conference's papers were published.[47] The European Conference of Churches held a conference on the same topic.[48] The Lutheran Council in the U.S.A., a cooperative agency of major Lutheran churches in that country, sponsored a conference on *reception*.[49] In the same year a symposium of Orthodox bishops and theologians met to discuss their response to *Baptism, Eucharist and Ministry*.[50]

Also in 1985, the Commission on Faith and Order of the World Council of Churches, along with several Christian world communions, sponsored a fourth forum on bilateral conversations.[51] The report of this forum provides an updating of dialogue activities since 1980, including the publication of reactions to *Baptism, Eucharist and Ministry*. A major part of the report, which notes some of the insights gained from the recent discussion of *reception,* is entitled "Emerging Features in the Response/Reception Process."[52] In it, response and *reception* are differentiated as terms and seen as part of an ongoing process. Responses by the churches to *Baptism, Eucharist and Ministry,* it is recognized, are not the same as the *reception* of their perspectives into the life of the churches; rather, response is an early step in the process of *reception.* The report also charges that the churches are being asked to reply to too

46. See Chapter 6 below for more on this topic.

47. *Journal of Ecumenical Studies* 21 (1984): 1-143.

48. *Ökumenische Rundschau* 35 (1986): 198-205.

49. *Journal of Ecumenical Studies* 22 (1985): 877-78.

50. *Greek Orthodox Theological Review* 30 (1985): 147-258.

51. *The Report of the Fourth Forum on Bilateral Conversations,* Faith and Order Paper 125 (Geneva: WCC, 1985).

52. *Report of the Fourth Forum,* pp. 14-16.

many dialogue reports too quickly, which hinders their true *reception* and embodiment in common worship, witness, and service.

The 1980s also saw the publication of a number of monographs and edited collections dealing with the theme of *reception*. To give just a select sample, in 1986 Hermann Brandt edited a volume that described the efforts at *reception* by a number of Lutheran churches in Germany in regard to the *Leuenberg Agreement/Concord* and the actions of the Lutheran World Federation. The volume gave attention to resources in Scripture and in the writings of the Lutheran Reformation helpful in understanding *reception*.[53] In 1988 I published my book on *reception* as an attempt to bridge the numerous articles being written on the subject and the lack of a major treatment of it in English.[54] In the same year Darlis J. Swan submitted to the faculty of The Catholic University of America a dissertation entitled *The Impact of the Bilateral Dialogues on Selected Religious Education Materials by the Lutheran Church in America,* which very helpfully described *reception* or the lack of it in a specific part of a specific church.[55] All these volumes contain extensive bibliographies that document the ever-increasing number of articles being published on the topic of *reception*.

This attention to *reception* did not abate in the next decade, although the scholarly research, generally speaking, was not of the same caliber. However, there were exceptions: in 1991 Wolfgang Beinert edited an important collection of essays on *reception* with the title *Glaube als Zustimmung: Zur Interpretation kirchlicher Rezeptionsvorgänge*.[56]

---

53. Hermann Brandt, ed., *Kirchliches Lehren in Ökumenischer Verpflichtung: Eine Studie zur Rezeption ökumenischer Dokumente* (Stuttgart: Calwer, 1986).

54. William G. Rusch, *Reception: An Ecumenical Opportunity* (Philadelphia: Fortress, 1988); published in German as *Rezeption: Eine ökumenische Chance* (Stuttgart: Kreuz, 1988).

55. Darlis J. Swan, *The Impact of the Bilateral Dialogues on Selected Religious Education Materials by the Lutheran Church in America* (Washington: University Microfilms International, 1988). It is unfortunate that this research has never been made available in a more convenient format, for it shows the gradual impact and *reception* of dialogue work on the education program of one church.

56. See note 20 above.

This noteworthy volume included essays by Beinert on *reception* and its importance for the life and teaching of the Church; by Hermann Josef Pottmeyer on *reception* and obedience; by Klaus Schatz on the *reception* of the early councils of the Church; and by Frank Ochmann on *reception* in canon law.

The year 1991 also saw the meeting of a joint staff group from the Pontifical Council for Promoting Christian Unity and the Office for Ecumenical Affairs of the Lutheran World Federation; the group produced a description and list of recommendations for *reception* by the churches.[57] This text of eight pages in English discusses the meaning of *reception,* acknowledges that it poses distinctive issues for both Lutherans and Roman Catholics, allows for local variation in the process of *reception,* and concludes with suggestions for ways to foster it.

In 1993 Sabine Pemsel-Maier published a volume, *Rezeption — Schwierigkeiten und Chancen.* In it she probes the challenges and opportunities for *reception* of the Lutheran–Roman Catholic dialogue and *Baptism, Eucharist and Ministry* on the popular level in Germany. The volume illustrates that the German churches gave the matter much more attention than did their counterparts elsewhere in the world.[58] That same year Frederick M. Bliss authored a book addressing questions of *reception* from a Roman Catholic perspective.[59] And Gilles Routhier published his *La réception d'un concile* — a work that, although primarily concerned with Vatican II, also has relevance for the *reception* of dialogues.[60]

Also in 1993 the Pontifical Council for Promoting Christian Unity

57. See "The Pontifical Council for Promoting Christian Unity," *Information Service* 80 (1992/II): 42-45. Also see *Strategies for Reception: Perspectives on the Reception of Documents emerging from the Lutheran-Catholic International Dialogue* (unpublished, 1991).

58. Sabine Pemsel-Maier, *Rezeption — Schwierigkeiten und Chancen: Eine Untersuchung zur Aufnahme und Umsetzung Ökumenischer Konsensdokumente in den Ortkirchen* (Würzburg: Echter Verlag, 1993).

59. Frederick M. Bliss, *Understanding Reception: A Background to Its Ecumenical Use* (Milwaukee: Marquette University Press, 1993).

60. Gilles Routhier, *La reception d'un concile* (Paris: Cerf, 1993).

published its ecumenical directory.[61] It takes up *reception* in a subsection addressing ecumenical dialogue, offering guidance to the Roman Catholic Church.[62] *Reception* there is portrayed as an ecclesiological concern, and the directory emphasizes the need for the special competence of theologians in its execution.

In 1994 the Sixth Forum on Bilateral Dialogues addressed the *reception* of ecumenical documents in three group reports, providing one of the most extensive statements about the subject to date. Topics discussed include aspects of *reception*, authority within the *reception* process in various churches and traditions, opportunities and difficulties in the present situation, and a series of recommendations. The work of this form clearly demonstrates the increasing significance of *reception* within the ecumenical movement by the mid-1990s.

Nineteen ninety-five was the year of Pope John Paul II's encyclical *Ut Unum Sint*, and in a section of that document he took up the question of *reception*.[63] The pope stresses the importance of the *reception* of the work of the dialogues, which must involve the whole people of God. The results of the dialogues cannot remain merely statements of their participants; rather they must become a common heritage. In this process, led by the Spirit and encouraged by bishops, theologians and faculties have specific responsibilities. The pope's comments on *reception* are not extensive, but their presence in the first papal encyclical to deal with ecumenism is worthy of special note.

That year also saw a conference at Farfa Sabina in Italy on the theme "Catholic-Lutheran Relations Three Decades After Vatican II."[64] A major section of the agenda of this conference was devoted to *reception,*

61. *Directory for the Application of Principles and Norms on Ecumenism* (Vatican City: Pontificium Consilium ad Christianorum Unitatem Fovendam, 1993).

62. For a description of this section of the study, see John A. Radano, "Response and Reception in the Catholic Church," *Midstream* 35:1 (1996):71-103; esp. pp. 72-75.

63. *Ut Unum Sint* (Vatican City: Libreria Editrice Vaticana, 1995), esp. pp. 91-92 §§80-81.

64. Peder Nøgaard-Højen, ed., *Catholic-Lutheran Relations Three Decades After Vatican II,* Studia Oecumenica Farfensia, Vol. I (Vatican City: Libreria Editrice Vaticana, 1997), esp. pp. 61-84.

with four presentations, including one by Cardinal Joseph Ratzinger, being given on the topic. These lectures took up the history of *reception* and the *reception* of the results of dialogue.

In 1996 an international colloquium took place at Salamanca, Spain, on the subject of *reception*. The findings of this meeting, the papers delivered there, and responses to those papers were published the following year.[65] A number of these essays deal directly with the *reception* of ecumenical documents and serve as a useful witness to debate on the topic in the late 1990s.

In 2002 Harald Goertz wrote a rather sober review of the *reception* of the Lutheran–Roman Catholic international dialogue in Germany.[66] He traces the understanding of *reception* in both the churches of the United Evangelical Lutheran Church of Germany and the Roman Catholic Church in Germany, perceiving more efforts for *reception* on the Lutheran side than on the Roman Catholic side.

Behind all these examples, which are selective but representative, we can perceive a desire for those involved in ecumenism to advance to a stage at which the goal is no longer the discovery of convergence or consensus, but rather the translation of theological agreements into the practice of living fellowship among the churches. The phases of this process — convergence, consensus, and *reception* — overlap, of course, and the challenge becomes one of shifting from a concentration of more dialogues to converting the agreements reached into some kind of fellowship or *communio* among the churches involved. With this goal, it is acknowledged that decisions must be made, where appropriate, to give the agreements the kind of authoritative character that will facilitate ecclesial fellowship.

Out of this cauldron of thought and action emerges a new category of *reception* that is shaped in the context of the ecumenical movement and that we can quite fittingly call *ecumenical reception*. It is to this new type of *reception* that we now turn.

---

65. Legrand et al., *La Recepción y la Comunión entre las Iglesias.*
66. Goertz, *Dialog und Rezeption: Die Rezeption evangelische-lutherische/römisch-katholisch Kirche.*

Chapter 5

The Emergence of *Ecumenical Reception*

A recurring theme in the bilateral ecumenical dialogues that have taken place since the 1960s is that of the need for translation of theological agreements into practical actions in the churches — in other words, the need for *reception*. At some point, dialogue needs to be converted into fellowship, and decisions need to be put into practice. This is what we mean when we talk about *ecumenical reception*.[1]

Classical Reception and *Ecumenical Reception*

As dialogues continued to meet, it continued to become clear that the meaning of *reception* was not always obvious; it shifted and expanded as

---

1. We should note that *ecumenical reception* differs significantly from another trend in ecumenical thinking and activity — that is, the creation of united churches through structured "organic" unity. This trend predominated until the 1960s, when the Roman Catholic Church entered the ecumenical movement, and it saw the creation of a number of united or uniting churches, for example in Canada, Japan, and India. This kind of unity, however important, is outside the purview of this book. See Michael Kinnamon, "United and Uniting Churches," in *Dictionary of the Ecumenical Movement,* 2d rev. ed., ed. N. Lossky, J. M. Bonino, J. Pobee, T. Stransky, G. Wainwright, and P. Webb (Geneva: WCC, 2002), pp. 1164-68.

context required. As early as 1984 John Zizioulas spoke of the "classical idea of reception" in contrast to the present ecumenical situation.[2] A year later, Gennadios Limouris picked up the same idea in a paper presented to an Orthodox symposium.[3] For our purposes in this volume, *classical reception* is *reception* as it was understood before the rise of the modern ecumenical movement; *ecumenical reception* is *reception* as it is understood since.

There are, to be sure, some similarities between the two concepts. It is often stated that *classical reception* took place in an undivided Church, whereas *ecumenical reception* is occurring among divided churches. But we do not do well to overly stress this point, for even divided churches share some commonality; otherwise dialogue would not be possible. More salient commonalities have been well documented by André Birmelé.[4] For example, the results of both the old councils and the new dialogues have called for *reception* within the churches of something produced outside the immediate life of the churches. And with both conciliar decisions and dialogue recommendations, the process of *reception* can be long and non-theological factors can play a role. Also, decisions of councils and dialogues are both the conclusion of a process of development in which a debated point is resolved. Both councils and dialogues build on theological research and the evolution of doctrine: they take up earlier views, often reformulate them, and announce a consensus when it is reached. In addition, councils and dialogues are not simply received in formal and juridical acts. Such acts are necessary, but so is acceptance on the part of the faithful. Finally, both *classical reception* and *ecumenical reception* thrive in an ecclesiology of *communio*, requiring an attitude of openness on the parts of churches. It should be obvious, therefore, that the disjunction between the two should not be drawn too widely.

2. John Zizioulas, "The Theological Problem of Reception," *Centro pro Unione Bulletin* 26 (1984): 4-6.

3. Gennadios Limouris, "The Physiognomy of BEM after Lime in the Present Ecumenical Situation," *Greek Orthodox Theological Review* 30/2 (1985): 138.

4. André Birmelé, "La reception comme exigence oecuménique" in *Communion et Réunion: Mélanges J.-M. R. Tillard,* ed. G. R. Evans and M. Gourgues (Louvain: Presses Universitaires de Louvain, 1995), pp. 78-82.

Having said all this, it is also undeniable that *ecumenical reception* also represents a point of non-continuity with earlier *reception* and takes on its own meanings and uses. To see this, we can briefly review some of the features of *classical reception* that we have discussed up to this point. First, *classical reception,* we noted, is mainly associated with councils of the Church and their decisions. It also has a history of association with canon law, where it came to be used primarily for the acceptance and consent given by the faithful to a particular conciliar or ecclesiastical decision. *Classical reception* was often a simple process, requiring the involvement of no juridically normative bodies apart from those already functioning in a spiritual and pastoral capacity, such as synods of bishops. *Classical reception* involved local churches receiving from one another. If verbal confessions or creeds were involved, in any given instance of *classical reception,* there was an understanding that in the final analysis what was received was the gospel itself. In *classical reception,* not individuals but churches as communities were the active participants. For the early Church, this meant that the local bishop played a key but not independent role in decisions to receive. Too, although it involved local churches, *classical reception* always had a universal dimension and required the concurrence of the Church catholic. *Classical reception* was permitted by the early Church to take different forms of expression in different contexts, and varying liturgies, texts of prayers, and formulations of doctrine were usually viewed as enriching the entire Church.

These factors throw into high relief the differences between *classical reception* and *ecumenical reception.* The context of *ecumenical reception* is not one united Church; instead, there are separated churches that are called to receive from one another. In this setting, what is sought is not simply doctrinal agreement, but mutual ecclesial *reception.* This raises numerous questions about the continuity of individual churches with the past, about the identification of the appropriate organs within these bodies for *reception,* and about how *reception* is possible within an incomplete or broken Eucharistic community. For the first time, churches are being asked to receive materials they did not directly produce. *Ecumenical reception* involves a fundamental sharing in the one apostolic faith —

but as it has been handed down in many communities of faith, not just one. The church communities are now struggling to reinterpret their common heritage with new language, new emphasis, and new insights, all acquired by participation in the one ecumenical movement. This kind of *reception* must take account of converging elements that the separated churches can confess together, as well as come to grips with painful questions that have divided the churches for centuries.

It is easy to see why *reception* of this nature presents a major challenge to the churches, causing heated debates and strained relations, sometimes even raising questions of identity. *Ecumenical reception* must be corporate, involving the coordination of many different persons and entities — theologians, parish clergy, and not least the faithful of the churches. It requires creativity. It requires the presence of structures and instruments that most churches did not possess prior to the advent of ecumenism. It must take place on local as well as wider levels (and unfortunately, local ecumenism is all too often ignored in dialogue processes). Documents to be received are usually created by specialists, though they must be accepted by laypeople; and they are usually created in dialogue, but must be accepted monologically (that is, within individual confessions). *Ecumenical reception* is also hindered by the absence of a final answer to the question of the models of unity: what would truly united churches look like?[5] And how much consensus is required in order to say that *reception* has taken place?[6] How can we document such a spiritual process? How will it vary from place to place — from Africa to Asia to North America, for example?[7]

---

5. Harding Meyer, *That All May Be One: Perceptions and Models of Ecumenicity* (Grand Rapids, Mich.: Eerdmans, 1999), pp. 7-15.

6. This is a question that can be asked intra-church as well as inter-church. A good example is the Second Vatican Council itself within the Roman Catholic Church; see Jean-Marie Tillard, "Did We Receive Vatican II?" *One in Christ* 4 (1985): 276-83.

7. This question goes back to inculturation; social and historical factors will no doubt play a role in *ecumenical reception*. For more on the challenges of *ecumenical reception* in general see William Henn, "The Reception of Ecumenical Documents," in *La Recepción y la Comunión entre las Iglesias,* ed. H. Legrand, J. Manzanares, and A. García y García (Salamanca: Universidad Pontificia, 1997), pp. 473-87.

And yet, amid all these difficulties, it is worth recalling the words of Dom Emmanuel Lane, spoken at the meeting of the Commission on Faith and Order in Lima during the time of the *ecumenical reception* of *Baptism, Eucharist and Ministry:* "It is . . . essential that all the churches should see their reception of this document concerns them at the very centre of their being. What is at stake here is the full communion which they desire to recover and the visible unity to which they are called."[8]

Defining *Ecumenical Reception*

In view of the factors just mentioned, it is not difficult to see why defining *ecumenical reception* has proven so arduous. Certainly the basic idea of *reception* is apparent enough.[9] But a precise and theoretical definition, in distinction from a merely operational one, is another matter. Yet without such a specific definition an exact analysis of the concept remains, if not impossible, then quite difficult. A number of authors on the subject have commented as much. Almost three decades ago W. Hryniewicz noted that for all the Orthodox attention to *reception,* there was no unanimous Orthodox interpretation of it.[10] Indeed, in the early years of the discussion of *ecumenical reception,* Richard Steward declared that he had met a person who refused to define *reception* in a paper because the reality did not completely exist![11] In 1990 Hermann Fischer spoke of *reception* as an *"ungreiffbar Begriff"* (an incomprehensible concept) and its process as an *ungreiffbar Prozeß* (an incomprehensible process); six years later Dorothea Wendebourg complained about an *Unübersichtlichkeit* (probably best rendered in English as "un-clarity") in regard to *reception.*[12]

8. Quoted in Michael Kinnamon, ed., *Towards Visible Unity: Commission on Faith and Order, 1982,* vol. 1, Faith and Order Paper 112 (Geneva: WCC, 1982), p. 53.

9. See Chapter 1 above.

10. Waclaw Hryniewicz, "Proces Recepcji Prawdy w Kosciele: Jego znaczenie hermeneutyczne I ekumeniczne," *Collectanea theologica* 48/2 (1975): 19-34.

11. Richard Steward, "Reception: What Do the Churches Do with Ecumenical Agreements?" *Centro pro Unione Bulletin* 25 (1984): 2.

12. Hermann Fischer, "Rezeption in ihrer Bedeutung für Leben und Lehre der

The Emergence of Ecumenical Reception

Over thirty years ago, as interest in the topic was growing, Jean M. R. Tillard offered some sound advice regarding a discussion of *reception*. He pointed out that reviving the word after so many years of neglect carried a certain danger.[13] If used without adequate concern for definition, he cautioned, the word could become an umbrella term or catchall — and words that mean everything ultimately mean nothing. The potential for *ecumenical reception* in the ecumenical movement will come to very little if *reception* is understood simply as the reestablishment of cordial relations.

In the context of these concerns, we can note several attempts to define *reception*. Those of Aloys Grillmeier and Yves Congar were presented in the last chapter.[14] Tillard's, offered in 1982, owes much to Congar's. He put it thus:

> What is meant by reception? Simply the approach by which an ecclesial body, judging that it *recognizes* there its own faith, *makes its own* a rule of faith, a specific doctrinal point, a norm which an authority of the Church has determined. It is not a matter of acquiescence, pure and simple, but of the welcoming that justifies the harmony between this which is proposed and that which one "knows" of the faith (often this is more a matter of instinct than of explicit science).[15]

Kirche: Vorläufige Erwägungen zu einem undeutlichen Begriff," *Zeitschrift für Theologie und Kirche* 87 (1990): 100-123, esp. pp. 100 and 103; and Dorothea Wendebourg, "Kirche und Rechfertigung: Ein Erlebnisbericht zu einem neueren ökumenischen Dokument," *Zeitschrift für Theologie und Kirche* 93 (1996): 84-100.

13. Jean M. R. Tillard, O.P., "'Reception': A Time to Beware of False Steps," *Ecumenical Trends* 14/10 (November 1985): 145-48.

14. See pp. 38-41.

15. B. Lauret and F. Refoulé, eds., *Initiation à la practique de la théologie*, vol. 1, *Introduction* (Paris: Cerf, 1982), pp. 165-66. The French text reads, "Qu'entendre . . . par reception? Simplement la démarche par laquelle le corps ecclesial. Jugeant qu'il y *reconâit* sa foi, *fait sienne* une règle de foi, une precision doctrinale, une norme qu' une instance d'Eglise a déterminée. Il ne s'agit pas d'un acquiescement pur et simple, mais de l'accueil que justifie l'harmonie entre ce qui est proposé et ce que l'on 'sait' de la foi (souvent plus d'instinct que de science explicite)."

At about the same time ARCIC, the Anglican–Roman Catholic International Commission, provided a definition of its own:

> By "reception" we mean the fact that the people of God acknowledge such a decision or statement because they recognize in it the apostolic faith. They accept it because they discern a harmony between what is proposed to them and the *sensus fidelium* of the whole Church. As an example, the creed which we call Nicene has been received by the church because in it the Church has recognized the apostolic faith. Reception does not create truth nor legitimize the decision: it is the final indication that such a decision has fulfilled the necessary conditions for it to be a true expression of the faith. In this acceptance the whole Church is involved in a continued process of discernment and response.[16]

Four years later the French Episcopal Conference of the Roman Catholic Church published a definition of *reception* as part of its response to a series of questions placed before it by the then-Secretariat for Promoting Christian Unity of the Vatican. This episcopal conference declared:

> Reception . . . is a datum which is noted afterwards. It generally goes beyond the limits of a generation because it enters progressively into the life and thought of the Church. It states a concrete notification that the people of God recognize the faith and define, in their manner of so doing, it to pass into the flesh and blood of ecclesial life. Reception enters into the concrete meaning of definition. It does not contradict it, to be sure, but it enriches it, uncovers the implications but also shows its limits and demonstrates this which will be needed to be completed or taken up again. This process concerns the entire body of the Church

---

16. Harding Meyer and Lukas Vischer, eds., *Growth in Agreement: Reports and Agreements of Ecumenical Conversations on a World Level* (New York: Paulist, 1984), p. 102.

and enters into this which ARCIC has well described as an exchange between doctrinal authority and the Christian people.[17]

I offered a preliminary definition of my own in 1988. Although I advised my readers to keep in mind that *ecumenical reception* was a novelty, in the sense that there is only an initial and partial experience of what this phenomenon is, I suggested we might think of it thus:

[Reception] include[s] all phases and aspects of an ongoing process by which a church under the guidance of God's Spirit makes the results of a bilateral or multilateral conversation a part of its faith and life because the results are seen to be in conformity with the teachings of Christ and of the apostolic community, that is, the gospel as witnessed to in Scripture.[18]

Finally, Gilles Routhier offered a definition that was very much focused on the conciliar context:

Reception is a spiritual process by which the decisions proposed by a council are received and assimilated into the life of a local church and become for that church a living expression of the apostolic faith.[19]

17. "Commission épiscopale française pour l'Unité des chrétiens à propos de l'évaluation du *Rapport final* de l'ARCIC I," *Documentation Catholique* 84 (1985): 875. The original French: "La réception . . . est une donné de fait qui se constate après coup. Elle dépasse généralment le cadre d'une generation parce qu'elle entre progressivement dans la vie et la pensée de l'Eglise. Elle dit la signification concrete que le People de Dieu à la fois reconnaît et confère à la definition, dans sa manière de la faire passer dans la chair et le sang de la vie ecclésiale. La reception entre dans le sens concret de la definition. Elle ne la contredit pas, bien sûr, mais elle l'enrichit, en dévole les implication mais aussi en manifeste les limites et montre ce qui aura besoin d'être complete ou repris. Ce processus intéress tout le corps de l'Eglise et entre dans ce que l'ARCIC a bien décrit comme un échange entre l'autorité doctrinale et le people chrétien."
18. William G. Rusch, *Reception: An Ecumenical Opportunity* (Philadelphia: Fortress, 1988), p. 31.
19. Gilles Routhier, *La reception d'un concile* (Paris: Cerf, 1993), p. 69. The original:

From the definitions offered above, we can see that the concept of *reception* is polysemous but not totally nebulous. Even at this early point in the history of *ecumenical reception* a number of clear characteristics emerge; they may be altered in the course of time, but it is not likely that they will be radically altered.

The Nature of *Ecumenical Reception*

This type of *reception* is one that has a theological rationale and an operational nature. It has steps and stages; it occurs in specific times and places, and involves certain actors. It is a process of assimilation, a process of common decision by particular churches, involving all their members and their different structures. It is neither merely a social nor democratic process, although we may certainly study it with the tools of the social and historical sciences. It recognizes the apostolic faith in new forms or accents. It does not bestow truth on any theological point; rather it confirms truth where it is found. Always it is an event of the Spirit.

Because *ecumenical reception* is inherently a process, it is critical to acknowledge that it will unfold in phases or stages. One useful distinction that has been proposed is the difference between initial response and final acceptance.[20] Aloys Grillmeier suggested three stages in the process of *reception:* kerygmatic *reception,* theological *reception,* and liturgical *reception.*[21] Lukas Vischer, in contrast, has offered two steps, kerygmatic and practical *reception.*[22] Johannes Willebrands has written of a process that will unfold and impact the kerygma, the didachè, and

---

"La reception est le processus spiritual par lequel les decisions proposes par un concil sont accuelies et assimilées dans la vie d'un Eglise locale et deviennet pour celle-ci une vivante expression de la foi apostolique."

20. Rusch, *Reception*, p. 67.

21. Aloys Grillmeier, "The Reception of Chalcedon in the Roman Catholic Church," *Ecumenical Review* 22 (1970): 393-97.

22. Lukas Vischer, "The Process of 'Reception' in the Ecumenical Movement," *Midstream* 23/3 (1984): 231.

the practice of piety in the churches.[23] All these references indicate, in spite of a certain flexibility in vocabulary, a recognition that *ecumenical reception* can only be understood as an ongoing process or trajectory.

Certainly all the definitions presented above would agree on this as well: the basis of *ecumenical reception* must be nothing less than the gospel itself, and its final standard must be the witness of Scripture. Truth must never be allowed to take a back seat to pragmatism or easy compromise. For this reason *ecumenical reception* will sometimes be an extremely difficult task, as those involved in it will have to grapple with the gospel itself and how the gospel is to be interpreted and proclaimed in new situations. Appealing to proof-texts and idealizing the past have no place in *ecumenical reception,* for this kind of *reception* insists that a lively new encounter with the gospel is the only standard for communion in the faith. Tillard puts it well: "It is not simply a question of a mental understanding *per se;* rather it is a question of mutual understanding based on the apostolic faith."[24]

In all this, it should be obvious that the churches themselves are the agents of *ecumenical reception.* Individual theologians and denominational leaders, both clergy and laity, will certainly make comments that will influence the churches as they engage in *ecumenical reception,* but the final choice to receive any ecumenically claimed agreement will be the churches' alone. This certainly adds to the complexity of the issue, for the churches in the early twenty-first century are divided about many issues, and it seems reasonable to assume that it will be more difficult for them to come together in an ecumenical council than it was for churches in the patristic period. In this sense, we cannot even think of the World Council of Churches as a council — it is an organization of churches in a stage prior to that of a genuine council.

As churches struggle to be true to this foundation for *ecumenical reception,* they will no doubt employ the standards that have been valuable to them throughout their lives. Lutherans and Reformed Christians will

23. J. Willebrands, "Ecumenical Dialogue and Its Reception," *Diakonia* 1-3 (1984-85): 123-24.

24. Tillard: "'Reception': A Time to Beware of False Steps," p. 146.

turn to confessions from the Reformation; the Orthodox will look to the traditions of the early Church; Roman Catholics will seek understanding from the binding dogmas of its history. As they endeavor to grasp the basis of *reception* they will be influenced by their structures of church life and their liturgical forms. All of this is as it should be — the challenge, of course, will be to be faithful to the witness of Scripture as interpreted by these other standards without letting those standards become barriers to ecumenical progress. Ecumenical agreements and convergences will force the churches under the gospel to reexamine their denominational criteria, and in the process there must be an openness to modification of positions previously held, an openness to both continuity and change. In the absence of such candor, genuine *ecumenical reception* will never be possible.

In addition to different standards, the separate churches have different structures and ways of ordering their lives. Not all structures serve equally well for the purpose of *ecumenical reception.* Churches that are strongly congregational in nature will in all likelihood have more difficulty with it than will those with a highly centralized structure. Whatever their structure, though, all the churches will confront new problems as they engage in *ecumenical reception,* accepting, modifying, and even declining ecumenical texts submitted to them. In some cases, official juridical action will probably be required; in others, *reception* may take place without it; we can exclude neither route to *ecumenical reception.*

Yet when official action takes place, it cannot be done in isolation. Before official, institutional action by church leadership occurs, a much more extensive process must take place. This process will be less formal and not restricted to decisions about texts. It will be gradual, at times almost imperceptible, and will help prepare the ground for the more formal acts that will lead to *ecumenical reception.* Part of this preliminary stage will involve new experiences and the discovery of new insights among the members of the churches. Old attitudes will change. Individual traditions will be seen by church members as part of a larger ecumenical context. Polemics of the past will be put aside. Ecumenical influences will be traced in educational programs and liturgical texts.

These things will happen as the results of ecumenical progress are communicated and interpreted within the churches. All of them might be considered early forms of *reception.*

However, without an active sharing of information, this initial phase of *ecumenical reception* will not occur — and neither, of course, will formal, full-fledged *ecumenical reception.* Irrespective of the organs of authoritative teaching in any given church, this preliminary stage must actively include the entire people of God — who, in turn, must accept the guidance of the Holy Spirit as they recognize and accept the gifts of the ecumenical movement. The late Cardinal Willebrands, when he was president of the Secretariat for Promoting Christian Unity, noted that, "In its full form reception embraces the official doctrine, its proclamation, the liturgy, the spiritual and ethical life of the faithful as well as theology as systematic reflection about this complex reality."[25] This assessment is not only accurate, but its appreciation is absolutely necessary for ecumenical advance. The churches are indeed agents of *ecumenical reception,* but only when "church" is understood in its widest sense — that is, as the baptized people of God. If "church" is limited to denominational leadership — whether in the form of a council of bishops, a convention, or a presbytery — *ecumenical reception* will be ineffective, unless it is rooted in a broad base of support. This, of course, means that we cannot chart the progress of *ecumenical reception* simply by tallying votes.[26] An official act, therefore, should never be seen as the endpoint of *ecumenical reception,* but rather as a step along the way — a step to be followed by renewal, fellowship, increased union among the churches, and always the possibility of further change down the road.

While it is true that *ecumenical reception* involves far more than the acceptance of text, we cannot overlook the fact that in most cases it is an ecumenical text that is the basis for *ecumenical reception.* It is with this

25. Johannes Cardinal Willebrands, *Address to the Convention of the Lutheran Church in America* (New York: Lutheran Church in America, 1984), p. 10.

26. See Routhier, *La reception d'un concile,* pp. 138-49. Routhier's comments are directed to conciliar *reception,* but they have a wider application.

in mind that such scholars as Ormond Rush and Linda Gaither have urged the application of the insights of literary reception theory to the process of *ecumenical reception*.[27] So doing, they contend, would facilitate active, intentional involvement between the text to be received and the receiver, and would provide a framework for interpreting such interactions. Rush, who finds especially relevant the work of Hans Robert Jauss, has sketched out fifteen theses that could be involved in this process as it relates to the *reception* of doctrine.[28] However, to this point it appears that such proposals, whatever theoretical benefits they have to offer, have had little impact on the real processes by which churches endeavor to receive ecumenical texts.[29]

Nevertheless, it is certainly worth wondering about the questions that would be raised by such an approach. For example, what is the exact meaning of an ecumenical agreement at any specific time or place if the text underlying that agreement is open to varying interpretations? Routhier has observed that *reception* as a legal term has been more influential than *reception* as a literary term in understanding *ecumenical reception,* and he suggests that this may be true at least in part because of the former's focus on the *bonum recipiendum* (the good to be received) versus the latter's emphasis on the public receiver. Despite this,

27. See Chapter 1 above.

28. Ormond Rush, *The Reception of Doctrine: An Appropriation of Hans Robert Jauss' Reception Aesthetics and Literary Hermeneutics* (Rome: Editrice Pontificia Università Gregoriana, 1997), pp. 359-64.

29. An exception worth noting may be the discussion and action after the approval of the Lutheran-Episcopal document *Called to Common Mission* in 1999. By the year 2000, both the Episcopal Church in the United States and the Evangelical Lutheran Church in America (ELCA) had approved this document as the basis to enter into a process that would lead them to a relationship of full communion, including the exchangeability of ministers. This agreement committed both churches to future ordinations by bishops in each church. However, in 2001 the ELCA broke, via an act of *non-reception,* its ecumenical commitment to one of the key provisions of the document, by creating a bylaw stating that its ordination of pastors could be done by a pastor in the church and not a bishop. See *Reports and Records: 2001 Churchwide Assembly* (Chicago: Evangelical Lutheran Church in America, 2002), pp. 125-33; 193-217, and in the same volume, "ELCA Constitution, 7.31.17: 'Ordination in Unusual Circumstances.'"

he maintains that both legal and literary theory have insights to contribute to *ecumenical reception*.[30]

When *ecumenical reception* is viewed as a process based on the gospel and including all the people of God, some of the artificial limits sometimes placed on it can be removed. For example, *ecumenical reception* is sometimes mischaracterized as an exercise of academic theologians from European and North American denominations. Even if we can understand how such a view arose — and of course we should express gratitude for the great work professional theologians have accomplished in this and other fields — it should not simply be taken for granted. Only when all elements of the churches act in harmony is *ecumenical reception* possible.

That is in large part why *ecumenical reception* poses such a challenge. Harmony of this kind has been rare in the history of the Church. All churches, whether Orthodox, Protestant, or Roman Catholic, insist upon the role of the faithful in decisions of faith. Yet in practice, either the hierarchies of the churches or the theological faculties have played an excessive if not monopolizing role. We have discussed this phenomenon with respect to the Roman Catholic Church following the First Vatican Council, but it is certainly not unique to Catholicism. *Ecumenical reception* will force all churches to rethink the active role of the people of God, as Orthodoxy and Protestantism will have to return to the sources of their traditions to seek ways in which to include all the faithful. Roman Catholicism has already embarked on an attempt with Vatican II — and in particular its constitution, *Lumen gentium* — but it, too, is only a beginning.

This active involvement of Christian believers in *ecumenical reception* will require reconceptualization of some fundamental views. The traditional understanding that divine revelation consists mainly in the disclosure of truths and teachings will have to be enriched with the insight that revelation is fundamentally the self-communication of God, which can be transmitted in many different ways. Faith, it must be understood, is a free charism belonging to all members of the Church. And

---

30. Routhier, *La reception d'un concile,* pp. 235-41.

as believers articulate their faith as recipients of God's revelation, it should be expected that their teaching will be presented in new forms and with new methods. The teaching will be linked directly with a concrete view of Christ's life and with concrete problems, needs, and longings. For example, the study of the Commission on Faith and Order entitled "Towards the Common Expression of the Apostolic Faith Today" showed that the matter is no longer as simple as the recitation of the Nicene-Constantinopolitan Creed of 381.[31] This creed will no doubt continue to hold a special place, but the study acknowledges early on the need for new ways of confessing the Christian faith — ways that facilitate the active involvement of all believers in the *reception* of ecumenical results. (This Faith and Order study, incidentally, did not result in much interest, offering an example of an ecumenical report largely not received in the churches.)

Ecumenical Reception in a Global Context

Among the believers who must be involved in *ecumenical reception* are those outside the churches of Europe and North America. Indeed, the Church is growing fastest outside these two continents. It is true that up to now dialogues have largely been the products of European and North American churches, but this is beginning to change. Both the text of *Baptism, Eucharist and Ministry* and the early study materials of "Towards the Common Expression of the Apostolic Faith Today" show the influences of the churches in Africa, Asia, and Latin America.[32]

The Roman Catholic Church has demonstrated its recognition of the importance of Christianity outside the North Atlantic in several

---

31. Hans-Georg Link, ed., *Apostolic Faith Today,* Faith and Order Paper 124 (Geneva: WCC, 1985); *Towards the Sharing of One Faith: A Study Guide for Discussion Groups,* Faith and Order Paper 173 (Geneva: WCC, 1986); *Confessing One Faith: A Guide for Ecumenical Study* (Cincinnati: Forward Movement Publications, 1988).

32. For example, see the official responses to *Baptism, Eucharist and Ministry* in Max Thurian, ed., *Churches Respond to BEM,* vols. 1-6, Faith and Order Papers 129, 132, 135, 137, 143, and 144 (Geneva: WCC, 1986-88).

ways. The Roman Catholic General Conference of Latin American Bishops met in Medellín, Colombia, in 1968 with Pope Paul VI present, and this meeting presents a clear case of the beginnings of the *reception* of Vatican II. This example of *reception* within one church provides some clues about what *ecumenical reception* will entail in a non-North American and non-European setting, and so it is worth considering in some detail.

The meeting at Medellín was seen at the time as a breakthrough for the way in which the Roman Catholic Church in Latin America, traditionally a passive receiver of doctrine, actively took initiative in light of Vatican II; in retrospect, we can see that it reflected strength, weakness, and immaturity. It produced a total of sixteen documents, all of which follow closely the methodology of *Gaudium et spes*, casting each document into a framework in which it first addressed relevant facts, then considered doctrinal contributions, and finally made pastoral recommendations.[33] Two documents, "Justice" and "Peace," are particularly strong in their call for liberation through nonviolent means. But "Justice" and "Peace" are often not related to the documents that speak about evangelization and church structure; and furthermore, at the time, their content was well in advance of the views of some bishops, priests, and laity. If Medellín provided an example of the beginning of the *reception* of the achievements of Vatican II, it also created the need for its own process of *reception,* a process which did not really come to fruition until the Third General Conference of Latin American Bishops at Puebla in 1979.[34]

The conference at Puebla, attended by Pope John Paul II, built upon Vatican II, Medellín, and Pope Paul VI's *Evangelii nuntiandi*. It aided the churches in Latin America to gain self-identity and to enter into dialogue, communion, and participation within their cultures. And it serves as a striking example of the participation of the laity — a remarkable fact for

33. For the teaching and methodology of *Gaudium et spes* see Norman Tanner, *The Church and the World: Gaudium et Spes, Inter Mirifica* (New York: Paulist, 2005), pp. 3-90.

34. For more on the conference in Medellín see Joseph Gremillion, ed., *The Church and Culture Since Vatican II* (Notre Dame, Ind.: University of Notre Dame Press, 1985), esp. pp. 56-68.

churches long characterized by clericalism. Indeed, involvement of the laity contributed much to the force of Puebla's call for preferential treatment for the poor in economics, politics, and evangelization.[35] Along with Medellín, Puebla offers clues for what *ecumenical reception* in a non-European and non-North American context will include: the active participation of the laity, a recognition of deep social needs and concerns, and an understanding and appreciation of cultural settings.

Wherever it takes place, a harmony of laity, church leadership, and theologians will be required, and the different structures of authority and decision-making in the churches will need to be respected. We should not expect the process to be the same in all the churches.

Ecumenical Reception as a Spiritual Process

As all churches endeavor to involve all these constituencies in the process of *ecumenical reception,* it becomes clear that all are being confronted with new questions — indeed, that it is sometimes not even clear what is being asked.[36] Confusion sometimes seems to reign as churches face *ecumenical reception* and church synods or conventions are asked to take the results of numerous ecumenical documents and studies and formulate official conclusions to dialogue results.[37] In all this, it is of the utmost importance to remember that *ecumenical reception* is a process that takes place under the guidance of God's Spirit.

The churches can indeed be open to *ecumenical reception* — but they must not conclude that they can orchestrate it, for it is in the end a

---

35. On the conference at Puebla, see Gremillion, *The Church and Culture Since Vatican II,* pp. 68-72 and 235-90; also John Eagleston and Philip Scharper, eds., *Puebla and Beyond: Documentation and Commentary,* trans. John Drury (Maryknoll: Orbis, 1979); and James A. Scherer, "A Lutheran Perspective on Mission and Evangelism in the Twentieth Century," in *Lutheran World Federation Report* 11-12 (Geneva: Lutheran World Federation, 1985), pp. 167-70.

36. See, for example, the several volumes of responses to *Baptism, Eucharist, and Ministry* in note 32 above.

37. See Chapter 6 below.

gift of the Spirit, and in its entirety it must be understood as such. The separated churches will welcome new and fresh expressions of the ecumenical movement and discoveries of their common faith only insofar as the Spirit makes this possible. As the churches struggle to take the results of the ecumenical movement and make them part of their faith and life, the gifts of the Spirit will be needed, as they have been throughout the history of Christianity. Openness to the present-day work of the Spirit is indispensable. Yet recognizing its spiritual character does not make *ecumenical reception* vague or abstract. Rather, it protects it from being viewed as merely a social process or as a democratic movement looking for a majority vote.[38]

The awareness that *ecumenical reception* operates under the Spirit keeps the churches open to a common fidelity to the mind and will of Christ himself. This *reception* becomes not more nebulous but more demanding, for it must reflect not a plebiscite in the churches but a willingness of one church to accept from other churches as churches. Hence *ecumenical reception* must never be limited to formal decisions by competent church leaders to accept the conclusions of an ecumenical dialogue as an adequate expression of the faith of a particular church. Genuine *ecumenical reception* will not occur if each church judges ecumenical results on the basis of how closely they conform to its own beliefs. It will happen as churches become increasingly aware of the work of the Holy Spirit in the ecumenical movement and in other churches.[39]

Thus *ecumenical reception* is a process that is both theological and spiritual, for the decisions taken by a church are finally accepted by its members not only because they are theologically correct but because they are seen as faithful to the gospel. The faithfulness of the decisions lies in their harmony with our responsibility to accept and hand on Christ in the power of the Spirit, who in turn is accepted from the Father. Lukas Vischer has declared that the churches need to develop nothing

38. See, for example, the comments of John Macquarrie in his *Theology, Church, and Ministry* (London: SCM, 1986), pp. 190-92.

39. See Emmanuel Sullivan, S.A., "Reception: Factor and Movement in Ecumenism," *Ecumenical Trends* 15/7 (July-August 1986): 107.

less than a spirituality of *reception*. For him this includes a receptivity to reforms and the development of structures of common authoritative decision-making.[40]

Ecumenical tasks will demand ecumenical formation. Such a formation is more than education and interpretation, important as those activities are; and more than tolerance or sharing, necessary as they too are. Rather, ecumenical formation can perhaps best be described as a quality of spirit. Until 1952 the churches in the ecumenical movement were largely called upon to develop an attitude of trust and tolerance, to form casual acquaintances. This was relatively easy. But ecumenical formation is far more difficult and threatening; it involves far more than polite recognition. It requires a will to accept the conclusions of the ecumenical movement and to take the churches beyond where they are now. The churches in the process of this ecumenical formation, driven by the excitement of claiming a convergence process that will finally lead under the Spirit to some form of visible unity, will have to develop principles for active ecumenical involvement, recognize the ecclesiality of other churches, and reformulate their theological thinking and understanding. Even ecumenical texts will need to be read differently, in a new spirit of openness and in accord with the method by which the texts were written. So *ecumenical reception* will call not only for information, but also for a formulation that affects theological thinking, spiritual understanding, and attitudes toward other churches — for in the end, it is the receiving of churches and people.[41] As such, it will summon churches to do certain things.

The Process of *Ecumenical Reception*

Whatever their differences, all the definitions of *ecumenical reception* we have considered so far agree that it is an ongoing process, and we

40. Lukas Vischer, "The Process of 'Reception' in the Ecumenical Movement," *Midstream* 23 (1984): 221-33 and esp. p. 233.

41. See Sullivan, "Reception," p. 108.

have seen this aspect borne out in the numerous examples we have considered. But just as the churches as the agents of this *reception* must be viewed in the broadest sense, so too must the process of this *reception* be understood broadly and not narrowly. Too often churches have perceived that *ecumenical reception* occurs in the time between the appointment of participants in a dialogue and the first reactions to the dialogue's final report. This, however, is far too limited a view, distorting the understanding of all the elements of the process that is *ecumenical reception*.

The initial stirrings of *ecumenical reception* begin long before any dialogue is conceived. They are to be found in that period of time when the churches break out of their isolation. When a particular church begins to perceive and to acknowledge that it is neither the sole bearer of Christian truth nor the only witness to Christian faith, *ecumenical reception* has already started to take place. Usually such a period of what we might call coexistence is followed by a time of cooperation, in which churches recognize one another as churches to the extent that they are prepared to undertake certain tasks together, typically in such areas as community service and around issues concerning social justice. These occasions present opportunities for limited forms of common prayer and study. There is, in other words, a real but limited partnership, which becomes the prerequisite for any fuller emergence of *ecumenical reception*.[42]

In these early stages there is usually no suggestion of dialogue. Indeed, the decision to enter into dialogue indicates that the process of *ecumenical reception* is already well underway. Genuine dialogue is based on separated churches, in varying degrees, acknowledging one another as Church, recognizing the positive contributions of one another to Christianity, and identifying specific obstacles to greater unity and understanding; the basis for all of these is the limited partnerships we just mentioned. Any choice to enter into dialogue is a major step forward into *ecumenical reception*.

No doubt ecumenical dialogues in the future will look somewhat dif-

---

42. See William G. Rusch, *Ecumenism: A Movement Toward Church Unity* (Philadelphia: Fortress, 1985), pp. 116-17.

ferent from those today, as new and better ways of ecumenical advance are found. Perhaps they will discuss more directly the divisive nature of certain ethical issues, which current dialogues have tended to avoid. Certainly they will move beyond conversations about Scripture, ministry, and ecclesiology. Probably dialogue participation will be expanded to include more than just professionally educated theologians. Already we can see some evidence for this change. And dialogue will likely be integrated with other ways of growing together — ways that will facilitate the involvement of churches that either are not well organized at world, regional, and national levels; or that do not possess a high regard for or a strong tradition of dogmatic theology, doctrinal decisions, and liturgical traditions. Such new ways are much needed; unfortunately, the last two decades have shown little evidence of creativity in dialogue activity, church councils on the whole seem to have become less effective, and few impressive breakthroughs have been seen. As new ways are found, they will certainly affect the process of *ecumenical reception*.

There is also still the tendency to see the final report of an ecumenical dialogue as its conclusion; this, too, is a situation in which the reality is much more complex. The completion of a dialogue report in fact opens a new phase of *ecumenical reception*. Dialogues, after all, point beyond themselves. This next phase involves translating theological agreements into practice in the living fellowship of the churches that have been represented in the dialogue. In the best circumstances these phases should have some overlap: a dialogue must not surrender the technical work it must do, but rather should aid its participating churches in taking hold of and evaluating its results.[43] Without sacrificing the technical detail necessary for theological advances, official reports must, by their content and style, encourage and facilitate *ecumenical reception*.[44] The participants in a dialogue cannot judge the dialogue's work for the churches; they must, rather, allow their work to

43. See Chapter 6 below; and John T. Ford and Darlis J. Swan, eds., *Twelve Tales Untold: A Study Guide for Ecumenical Reception* (Grand Rapids, Mich.: Eerdmans, 1993).

44. *Baptism, Eucharist and Ministry* is an excellent example of a report that encourages *ecumenical reception* in its language. See, e.g., "Baptism," §8, 12-14; "Eucharist," §1, 2, 21, 30, 32; "Ministry" §5, 7, 14, 16, 20, 27, 40.

stand on its own. Yet there may be ways not yet tapped by which dialogue members can be a resource for the evaluation of their work. Such ways may include the preparation of study materials, the writing of commentaries by individual dialogue members, and the participation of dialogue members in educational and interpretive events. Any of these options has the potential to utilize more vitally the experience and knowledge of a dialogue's participants.

Already it seems evident that after a major ecumenical document is produced, a stage of response, or what might be called partial or preliminary *reception,* typically occurs. This initial response consists of the first official word from a church about an ecumenical document; far from signaling the conclusion of *ecumenical reception,* it rather serves as a good indicator of how the process is going to proceed. On the one hand, a positive response is likely to result in efforts to put the results of a dialogue into practice; on the other, a negative or lukewarm response may delay or even prevent further *ecumenical reception.* Of course, an initial negative response need not be permanent; with time and further reflection, a church may come to find that its initial questions are answered and its reservations are overcome. Such, after all, was the case with the First and Second Councils of Nicea and the Council of Chalcedon.

The proliferation of responses to *Baptism, Eucharist and Ministry* in the years after its publication demonstrates the process-oriented nature of *ecumenical reception* at this stage. Rarely do any of the responses consist of a simple vote of approval or disapproval. Rather, criticism, affirmation, and modification are offered simultaneously. Even the most positive responses typically temper their words of encouragement with caveats. And this is to be expected, for in *ecumenical reception* churches are not accepting documents; rather, they are accepting one another. They are seeking behind the texts a common conviction that they share the same gospel, the same apostolic faith. No doubt a step beyond early *ecumenical reception* will be the further refinement of existing texts or the addition of new texts to give clarity to older ones.[45]

45. This phenomenon can already be seen in the *Joint Declaration on the Doctrine of Justification* that we will discuss in the next chapter.

At present, the stage of response or preliminary *reception* is just beginning in many churches and in many parts of the ecumenical movement. The ultimate goal of *ecumenical reception* — the full communion of separated churches — lies farther ahead. Although the realization of this goal has yet to happen, there is a growing awareness of what it will entail. It will not involve passive acceptance; it will not be a popularity contest; it will not consist of churches surrendering their identities. Rather, it will call for active participation on intellectual, spiritual, and practical levels. It will demand change and renewal in the churches. *Ecumenical reception* as a gift of God's Spirit will have occurred within and among churches when a communion exists that is rooted in a confession of the one faith, a mutual recognition of churches, a common sacramental life, and a mutually committed community of spiritual life, expressed in witness, service, and conciliar consultation.

So again: *ecumenical reception* will never be easy. When churches are concerned with it, they are involved at the core of their being. No church should lightly entertain the idea of *ecumenical reception*. Major issues of Christian faith — including views of Church, ministry, and authority — will be drawn into its ongoing process. Churches will be forced to grapple with how to remain true to their own traditions even as they cultivate openness to the *reception* of results that do not simply reflect their own views.

The process of *ecumenical reception* will be aided when individual denominations can begin to recognize that some of these ecumenical teachings that at first glance appear out of harmony with their traditional teachings are not alien to them, but rather have been forgotten, obscured, or simply not emphasized in the course of history; here the discipline of historical theology will prove invaluable. It is useful for churches to appreciate that ecumenical statements can often help correct one-sidedness or weakness in the individual traditions, and that no tradition is incapable of benefiting from this corrective effect. All churches can benefit from asking whether there is a hiatus between their official doctrine and their practice.

Yet not all churches can or will engage in this strenuous process with the same degree of commitment or enthusiasm; *ecumenical recep-*

tion, therefore, is bound to be a centuries-long process, as *reception* always has been in the Church. And it is bound, at some points, to create new divisions even as it heals old ones. The Council of Chalcedon and the *reception* of its conclusions by some churches resolved a longstanding Christological dispute. It created a unity. But at the same time it caused a disunity that is still not totally healed today. Similar rifts may arise today within confessional families whose members do not all agree on the pace or even the need for *ecumenical reception,* even as greater unity is created across traditional lines.[46]

A final note: before moving on, we should acknowledge briefly that many "non-theological" factors can influence *ecumenical reception* as well. For example, some churches with the same confessional standards have offered very different responses to *Baptism, Eucharist and Ministry.* Among these factors have been the position of a responding church as a minority or a majority, as well as its status as a Volkskirche or a state church. Even the identity of the chief ecumenical partners in a local situation can affect the character of *ecumenical reception.* Is the predominant in a given context Roman Catholic, Orthodox, or Protestant? What has its history of external relations been? These factors are not unimportant and will in many cases affect the outcome of *ecumenical reception.*[47]

Three Tasks of *Ecumenical Reception*

As *ecumenical reception* continues within and among the churches, we can distinguish at least three tasks essential to its success. First of all, there is *reception* in the narrow sense. In other words, where those representatives they have deputed to ecumenical dialogues have found consensus and convergence, the churches need to respond with ecclesial convergence and consensus. If a church concludes that a particular ecu-

46. An example of this is the Lutheran-Episcopal agreements in the United States, which we will consider in the next chapter.

47. Two useful articles by Günther Gassmann on this aspect of *ecumenical reception* are "Rezeption im 'ökumenischen Kontext,'" *Ökumenische Rundschau* 26 (1974): 314-327 and "Die Rezeption der Dialoge," *Ökumenische Rundschau* 33 (1984): 357-368.

menical teaching is indeed a faithful witness to the gospel, it must be willing to make it not only formally but also realistically and practically a part of its faith and life, even if the teaching speaks in a strange accent to that church's tradition. Until this is accomplished, *reception* in the broader sense will be stalled. Some ecumenical scholars are convinced that dialogues have already solved the major issues that have kept the churches apart for centuries. If this is an overly optimistic view, it nevertheless contains at least a germ of truth: the challenge at this point is not to find solutions, but to have the solutions that have been found become decisive in the churches. This raises for the churches the question of what degree of pluralism or even disagreement is acceptable to them. Only the churches can answer this question, but the progress of *ecumenical reception* depends on their answer.

A second task of *ecumenical reception* could be called non-*reception*. This may sound contradictory, but what it refers to is a reconsideration and rejection by the churches of those portions of their faith and life that obscure or distort the gospel as it has been understood and proclaimed through the centuries. Every tradition has its peculiarities, many of which arose in moments of polemic and heated disagreement. Although at the time of their creation they may have been part of the clear identification of the gospel, emphatically countering a particular false teaching, in a new time and context such teachings too often obstruct the gospel. Consider, for example, the many mutual anathemas proclaimed between churches in their attempts to safeguard the gospel. Such strong pronouncements can continue to be salutary warnings from the past, but many no longer speak to real church-dividing issues today. In order to promote *ecumenical reception,* churches should embark on a process of non-receiving or un-receiving these hindrances, declaring the non-applicability of outmoded condemnations in the expressions of their faith and life. This is what the Leuenberg Agreement, for example, asked the Lutheran and Reformed Churches in Germany to do.[48] And it was a step leading to the *Joint*

48. See §B.III of the Leuenberg Agreement, reproduced in James E. Andrews and Joseph A. Burgess, eds., *An Invitation to Action* (Philadelphia: Fortress, 1984), pp. 68-70.

Declaration on the Doctrine of Justification between the Lutheran and Roman Catholic Churches.[49]

A third task of *ecumenical reception* may also not sound like *reception,* although it is. This is the process of de-*reception.* The difference between de-*reception* and non-*reception* may seem artificial, but a distinction exists. It lies in the possibility of differentiating between beliefs and practices in the individual traditions that obscure or distort the gospel (this is what non-*reception* aims to remove); and beliefs and practices that, though the gospel is not at stake, hinder the visible unity of the Church (this is what de-*reception* aims to remove). Into the latter category fall, for example, those things that Lutherans and others have described as "adiaphora."[50] Although there has been, and continues to be, disagreement about exactly what are and remain adiaphora, every Christian tradition should recognize the importance of identifying them. When adiaphora make it more difficult for churches to manifest their visible unity, they must be de-received by the churches. To cite just one example, the Roman Catholic participants in the Lutheran–Roman Catholic dialogue in the United States spoke of changes in papal leadership designed to reflect the collegial aspect of church leadership and a view of the pope as a servant of God rather than as an absolute monarch.[51] As all churches identify adiaphora in their lives and begin to de-receive them, *ecumenical reception* will proceed unhindered.

The discussion of these last two tasks, non-*reception* and de-*reception,* should not lead to the conclusion that complete uniformity among the churches is necessary for *ecumenical reception* to advance. Whatever the final models of church unity turn out to be, they will certainly incorporate diversity. This diversity will result at least in part from churches choosing not to non-receive and de-receive certain as-

49. See Chapter 6 below.

50. For Lutherans, key texts on this subject include Article 15 of the Augsbug Confession and Article 10 of the Formula of Concord. See Robert Kolb and Timothy J. Wengert, eds., *The Book of Concord: The Confessions of the Evangelical Lutheran Church* (Minneapolis: Fortress, 2000), pp. 48-49, 515-16, and 635-40.

51. See Paul C. Empie and T. Austin Murphy, eds., *Primacy and the Universal Church: Lutherans and Catholics in Dialogue V* (Minneapolis: Augsburg, 1974), pp. 27-28, 37.

pects of their traditions. This need not be a hindrance to greater unity, however, if what is kept is recognized as appropriate to the life of a specific church, and if other churches can agree that it is not contrary to the gospel. There exists a certain hierarchy of importance in church teachings. And while its exact rankings would certainly be cause for discussion, most churches would agree that doctrines of the Trinity and Christology are central to and foundational for Christianity. Thus agreement in these areas and the *reception* of this agreement by churches are more important for the ongoing process of *ecumenical reception* than are non-*reception* and de-*reception* in other areas. The life of the early Church can provide some useful models in this regard, for there are abundant examples from that period of different churches with divergent liturgies and theologies living in profound communion because they did not consider their areas of disagreement to affect their common allegiance to the foundational truths of Christianity.

As the churches engage in the process of *ecumenical reception,* their rate of progress will depend in part upon what they are asked to receive from other churches. Beliefs and ways of life that seem most compatible to a receiving church will naturally be accepted with less difficulty than those which are strange or which initially appear hostile. Lutheran and Reformed churches, for example, should have little problem in receiving the work of their dialogues on justification by grace through faith; each tradition should hear what in the other is compatible with, and similar to, its own position. On the other hand, Lutherans will have more difficulty in receiving certain recommendations of their national and international dialogues with Roman Catholics when they are asked to alter some of their earlier judgments about the papacy. Likewise, *ecumenical reception* of some of the teachings of Martin Luther that are recommended by the same dialogues will encounter obstacles among Roman Catholics. And recommendations to accept the historic episcopacy in a threefold structure will no doubt be difficult for churches in the Reformed tradition to receive.

Ecumenical Reception and Inculturation

In Chapter 1 we mentioned a parallel between the basic notion of *reception* and the concept of inculturation. Here something should be indicated about the relationship of *ecumenical reception* and inculturation. If the latter has to do with the expression of the Christian faith in different cultures from those in which the faith was first expressed, *ecumenical reception* is in some ways similar. Inculturation raises questions of how black Africans or native South Americans must take responsibility for Africanizing or South Americanizing Christianity. In a manner that is somewhat similar, *ecumenical reception* asks Lutheran Christians to receive and integrate some aspects of Anglican and Roman Catholic Christianity into their particular tradition, and vice versa. Probably the parallels should not be pushed too far, but *ecumenical reception* may gain if those responsible for it give some attention to the growing literature about inculturation.[52]

Ecumenical Reception and Recognition

Before concluding this chapter, we should say something about the relation of *ecumenical reception* to the theological concept of recognition.

52. See, e.g., Amy R. Crollius, "What Is New About Inculturation? A Concept and Its Implications," *Gregorianum* 59 (1978): 721-738; Johannes Mühsteiger, "Rezeption-Inkulturation-Selbestimmung," *Zeitschrift für katholische Theologie* 105 (1983): 261-289; Hans B. Meyer, "Zur Frage der Inkulturation der Liturgie," *Zeitschrift für katholische Theologie* 105 (1983): 1-31; Lamin Sanneh, *Whose Religion Is Christianity? The Gospel Beyond the West* (Grand Rapids, Mich.: Eerdmans, 2003); and John Waliggo, "Inculturation," in *Dictionary of the Ecumenical Movement*, 2d. ed., ed. N. Lossky, J. M. Bonino, J. Pobee, T. F. Stransky, G. Wainwright, and P. Webb (Geneva: WCC, 2000), pp. 571-72.

Gilles Routhier edited a recent volume that deals with the *reception* of Vatican II in various contexts. While the subject of the work is not, strictly speaking, *ecumenical reception*, but rather *reception* within the Roman Catholic Church of its own council, the various chapters are a comprehensive study of *reception* in different cultural and theological settings. See Gilles Routhier, ed., *Réceptions de Vatican II: Le Concile au risqué de l'histoire et des espaces humains* (Leuven: Peeters, 2004).

Understandings of this relation have differed, with the question in its most basic form being, which comes first — *ecumenical reception* or recognition?

Recognition has a history of its own in the ecumenical movement.[53] Already at the first World Conference on Faith and Order, held in Lausanne in 1927, issues of unity and diversity were obvious. There was not yet a precisely agreed upon meaning for concepts such as "complete fellowship in the Church," "complete unity," and "complete union," though all of them appear in the report of the Conference. Behind all these concepts was an understanding that there will have to be diversity in the unity of the one Church, but this diversity was not addressed in 1927. Still, the Lausanne report does verbalize the hope "that the Churches be so transformed that there may be full recognition of one another by members of all communions."[54]

In the preconference material for the next World Conference of Faith and Order, held at Edinburgh in 1937, "mutual recognition" designated a particular understanding of unity that did not find its way, for some reason, into the report of the Conference itself. This understanding had three components: the interchange of membership; mutual recognition and exchangeability of clergy; and intercommunion. This last concept is easily the most significant expression of "unity in mutual recognition," which in turn leads to the others in "recognition of member-

---

53. See Harding Meyer, "'Anerkennung' — Ein ökumenischer Schüsselbegriff," in *Dialog und Anerkennung,* ed. Peter Mann (Frankfurt: Verlag Otto Lembeck, 1980), pp. 25-41; William G. Rusch, "'Recognition' as an Ecumenical Concept in the Lutheran-Episcopal Dialogue," *Midstream* XXX/4 (1991): 316-322; and Gerard Kelly, *Recognition: Advancing Ecumenical Thinking,* American University Studies, Series VII, Vol. 186 (New York: Peter Lang, 1996).

54. See H. N. Bate, ed., *Faith and Order: Proceedings of the World Conference, Lausanne, August 3-21, 1927* (London: SCM, 1927), pp. 459-75. In the documents received by the conference for transmission to the churches are numerous references to "recognize." See also G. K. A. Bell, ed., *Documents on Christian Unity,* vol. 1 (Oxford: Oxford University Press, 1955), p. 179. This last reference is to the document entitled "The Unity of Christendom and the Relation Thereto of Existing Churches," transmitted to the churches after the conclusion of the conference.

ship, ministry, sacraments, and faith."[55] This indicates the kind of thinking that was taking place in the wake of Lausanne.[56]

Two other early texts from the World Council of Churches are relevant to this discussion: the Toronto Statement of 1950 and the Lund Report of the World Conference on Faith and Order in 1952. The former, a document from the Central Committee of the Council, raises the question of how far membership in the World Council implies mutual recognition as churches of all members. It notes that some churches recognize one another fully and truly; others, more guardedly, "recognize one another as those who serve the Lord." In both cases, the statement continues, "[t]he member churches of the World Council recognize in the other churches elements of the true church. They are of the opinion that mutual recognition, to which they are committed, is to be pursued in a serious discussion."[57] The Lund Report, in its section entitled "Unity and Diversity," likewise speaks of "the different steps of mutual recognition."[58] It does not, however, offer any specific schema for what these steps might entail.

In Chapter 4, we mentioned a number of studies of *reception* by the World Council of Churches in view of the Second Vatican Council. In one of these essays Werner Küppers described the conciliar process in terms of both *reception* and recognition. Küppers saw recognition as an ecclesial idea rather than as merely a canonical or juridical act. His work influenced the meeting of the Faith and Order Commission in Bristol is 1967, which in turn encouraged further study of recognition and the *reception* of councils.[59]

55. *The Meanings of Unity,* Faith and Order Paper 1 (New York: Harper, 1937).

56. See *The Meanings of Unity* for more on this topic.

57. This material may be found in Lukas Vischer, ed., *Die Einheit der Kirch Material der ökumenischen Bewegung* (Munich: Theologische Bücherei, 1965), p. 257.

58. Oliver S. Tomkins, ed., *The Third World Conference of Faith and Order Held at Lund, August 15th to 28th, 1952* (London: SCM, 1953), p. 37.

59. Werner Küppers, "Reception. Prolegomena to a Systematic Study," *Councils and the Ecumenical Movement 94* and *New Directions in Faith and Order, Bristol, 1967: Reports — Minutes — Documents,* Faith and Order Paper 50 (Geneva: WCC, 1968), p. 153. See also the references to Küppers' work in Chapter 4.

In 1973 the Commission on Faith and Order held a consultation in Salamanca on concepts and models of unity. The report of this meeting used the concept of recognition in a number of ways. Depending on context, it could refer to acknowledgment of churches as churches, acknowledgment of members and ministries, recognition of the apostolic faith, or recognition of Eucharistic celebrations among churches.[60]

Such statements about recognition had their influence at two assemblies of the World Council of Churches, at New Delhi in 1961 and at Nairobi in 1975. At New Delhi the Council declared that the goal of ecumenism is "one fully committed fellowship" of all Christians "in each place." This fellowship requires "that ministry and members are accepted."[61] The assembly in Nairobi used "recognition" twice as it further defined conciliar fellowship: "Each local church . . . recognizes the others as belonging to the same church of Christ and guided by the same Spirit . . . they recognize each other's members and ministries."[62] The Nairobi Assembly also endorsed in full the report of the Salamanca Consultation two years prior.

In 1982 the Commission on Faith and Order completed its work on the text of *Baptism, Eucharist and Ministry.* The preface of that text makes it clear that recognition of the Christian tradition and a communion among churches is central to its purposes, asking the churches to what extent they can recognize in the text the faith of the Church through the ages. Likewise, the section on ministry encourages the churches to recognize one another's ministries.[63]

In 1984 the international Lutheran–Roman Catholic dialogue issued its report *Facing Unity.* This bilateral report, deeply influenced by the work of Harding Meyer, saw recognition as an essential part of the process leading to church fellowship. Recognition should function, it

60. "The Unity of the Church — Next Steps: Report of the Salamanca Consultation on 'Concepts of Unity and Models of Union,'" *Ecumenical Review* 26 (1974): 293-298.

61. W. A. Visser t' Hooft, ed., *The New Delhi Report: The Third Assembly of the World Council of Churches, 1961* (London: SCM, 1962), p. 116.

62. David M. Paton, ed., *Breaking the Barriers: Nairobi, 1975* (London: SPCK, 1976), p. 60.

63. *Baptism, Eucharist and Ministry,* Preface, and "Ministry" §51-55.

contended, in tandem with *reception,* with the former leading to the latter.[64] The idea is clear that *ecumenical reception* is only possible if the legitimacy and authenticity of the dialogue partner is recognized; *reception* and recognition can only function where there is a vision of unity in diversity.

When the Commission on Faith and Order met in Stravanger, Norway, in 1985, there was discussion about both *reception* and recognition. However, the terms *classical reception* and *ecumenical reception* were not employed, and it now seems clear that there was a lack of clarity in regard to vocabulary, particularly in the distinction or lack thereof among "response," "recognition," and *"reception."*[65] In part this is due to the variety of responses from the churches to *Baptism, Eucharist and Ministry,* one collective result of which was to make the Commission less sure of the nature and purpose of recognition than it had been three years earlier in Lima, when it had deemed that the text was sufficiently mature to send to the churches. The Commission continued to reflect on recognition in the light of *Baptism, Eucharist and Ministry* at its meeting in Budapest in 1989.

Recognition was also taken up in the Commission's discussion of another study, "Confessing the One Faith." This text focused on the question of whether the churches could recognize the Nicene-Constantinopolitan Creed as an ecumenical statement of the one apostolic faith. This text saw recognition as a task for the churches that was clearly distinct from *ecumenical reception.*[66] It was no doubt influenced by the thought of Jean-Marie Tillard, who regarded recognition between churches not as canonical *reception* but as an acknowledgment of

64. "Facing Unity: Models, Forms, and Phases of Catholic-Lutheran Church Fellowship," esp. article 49 and n. 47, in *Growth in Agreement II,* ed. Gros, Meyer, and Rusch, pp. 443-84.

65. Thomas F. Best, ed., *Faith and Renewal: Reports and Documents of the Commission on Faith and Order, Stravanger, 1985,* Faith and Order Paper 131 (Geneva: WCC, 1986); and Gerard Kelly, *Recognition: Advancing Ecumenical Thinking,* pp. 194-95.

66. *Confessing the One Faith: Towards an Ecumenical Explication of the Apostolic Faith as Expressed in the Nicene-Constantinopolitan Creed (381),* Faith and Order Paper 140 (Geneva: WCC, 1987).

a communion that already exists and as a means of deepening that communion so that a formal act of *reception* can occur in the future.[67]

The Seventh Assembly of the World Council of Churches met in Canberra in 1991 and released a statement, "The Unity of the Church as Koinonia: Gift and Calling." This text, with its strong Trinitarian stress, spoke of the unity of the Church as a koinonia given and expressed in one baptism and one Eucharistic fellowship, and a common life in which members and ministries are mutually recognized and reconciled. It is declared that the goal of full communion is released when all churches are able to recognize in each other the one, holy, catholic, and apostolic Church in all its fullness.[68]

The Fifth World Conference on Faith and Order met in Santiago de Compostela, Spain, in 1993. This Conference asserted that the purpose of recognition was to assist the churches to be faithful to the apostolic faith and to work together towards complete koinonia. It was seen as a theological concept, not merely a juridical one, and as an instrument to be employed by the churches.[69]

From this survey, it should be clear that thought about recognition has been for many years an integral component of ecumenical thought and terminology. Its primary purpose has been to allow for positive relations between divided churches and to be a way toward fuller communion. Until recently, its primary focus has not been on the recognition of texts; however, this does not mean that the recognition of documents brings a radically new idea into the ecumenical discussion. The fundamental issue in the recognition of documents, after all, is not the documents themselves but the faith expressed and the churches reflected in them. Here there is a clear parallel with *ecumenical reception.*

The more recent features of the discussion of recognition stand in continuity with earlier ones, just as *ecumenical reception* is not a com-

67. See Kelly, *Recognition: Advancing Ecumenical Thinking,* p. 204.

68. See Michael Kinnamon, ed., *Signs of the Spirit: Official Report, Seventh Assembly, Canberra, Australia, 7-20 February 1991* (Geneva: WCC, 1991), pp. 172-74.

69. Thomas F. Best and Günther Gassmann, eds., *On the Way to Fuller Koinonia: Official Report of the Fifth World Conference on Faith and Order,* Faith and Order Paper 166 (Geneva: WCC, 1994), pp. 237-40.

plete departure from *classical reception.* The basic issue with recognition is how churches are to be able to recognize other churches as Church, so as to allow for full communion or visible unity between them. Here again, a parallel can be seen with *ecumenical reception,* wherein the final goal is to allow the churches to receive one another fully and with integrity as Church.

Even a brief overview of the use of recognition in ecumenical literature highlights a number of its characteristics. It can refer either to individual components in the life of the Church — sacraments, persons, confessions — or it can refer to churches as a whole. It can be gradual or dynamic. It is primarily a spiritual process, although it is not without legal aspects. It involves the question of legitimacy, in that what is recognized by the divided churches is considered authentic. Recognition functions in the context of unity in diversity, seeking an ecumenical path between the tendency to remove all difference and the opposing inclination to settle for mere coexistence or cooperation. It affirms a certain "otherness," resisting the urges to take over, to adopt, or to take possession. It is an ongoing process, and so it is likely to be mentioned and promoted in ecumenism's future.

All of this suggests an intimate relationship between *ecumenical reception* and recognition. As we mentioned above, this relationship requires further exploration. Elsewhere I have made the argument that *ecumenical reception* when successful should result in recognition.[70] If divided churches are able to receive fully the positive conclusions of their ecumenical dialogues with other churches, then these churches should be able to recognize those other churches as fully Church. Therefore they should be able to enter into full communion with them. As the above survey discloses, this view is present in a number of ecumenical texts.

The shift to a theological understanding of recognition is an important development in ecumenical theology.[71] It means that when

70. William G. Rusch, "Recognition as an Ecumenical Concept in the Lutheran-Episcopal Dialogue."

71. Gerard Kelly documents this shift in *Recognition: Advancing Ecumenical Thinking,* pp. 219-20.

churches are able to recognize in each other the fullness of the apostolic faith and witness they can recognize and receive each other as fully Church. The instrument of this may be dialogue texts or something else. Of course, there remain questions to be answered, such as what the criteria are for recognizing the apostolic faith and what their theological bases are. Nevertheless, the significance of the processes of recognizing and receiving is that at the conclusion of them, divided churches under the guidance of the Spirit will have attained full visible unity.[72]

While this ultimate ecumenical goal lies in the future and in the providence of the Triune God, we can in the present moment ask to what degree there is evidence that the churches have entered into the process of *ecumenical reception*. This inquiry will be the subject of the following chapter.

72. See Aloys Klein, "Rezeption der ökumenischen Dialogue," in *Iustus Iudex: Festgabe für Paul Wesemann zum 75. Geburtsdag von seinem Freunden und Schülern,* ed. K. Lüdicke, H. Mussinghoff, and H. Schwendenwein (Essen: Ludgerus-Verlag, 1990), pp. 30-39, esp. pp. 38-39.

Chapter 6

Examples of *Ecumenical Reception*

In the preceding chapters we have seen that *ecumenical reception* is possessed of a polysemous nature. In light of this, it makes sense to ask how we can know it has taken place in any given situation. The answer to this question is neither simple nor obvious; indeed, there are few cases in the ecumenical movement in which it seems altogether safe to declare that *ecumenical reception* has taken place and some divisive factor has been irrevocably and positively changed between two churches. Like *classical reception* within a single church, *ecumenical reception* between churches is a long — sometimes centuries-long — process, and it cannot be equated with a particular juridical action. Nevertheless, with these caveats in mind, it is possible to indicate some emerging instances of *ecumenical reception.* The select illustrations we will consider in this chapter are all preliminary or partial, but they are hopeful indicators of *ecumenical reception* all the same.

Involvement in the Ecumenical Movement

The most fundamental signal that *ecumenical reception* is beginning to take place is simply the participation of a large number of churches in the modern ecumenical movement. When we tally the membership of churches in local, regional, national, and international councils of churches, whatever their varying names, we can see that impressive numbers of churches have been willing to identify themselves with a movement that seeks the visible unity of divided Christians and their churches. Admittedly some churches are hesitant to commit to such movements, whether formally or informally. And the rhetoric of crisis in the ecumenical movement has been on the rise in recent years, with churches and individuals expressing concern about the loss of ecumenical goals and vision.[1] Internal pressures, if not emerging splits, within individual churches have caused many churches, especially Protestant churches, to focus their attention inward rather than outward. All of this notwithstanding, there has been no wholesale withdrawal from the instruments of the ecumenical movement with the dawn of the twenty-first century. To the contrary, there is some evidence that churches formerly hostile to the movement have somewhat modified their position.[2]

This participation is not only observable in the membership rolls of ecumenical organizations; it can also be detected in the involvement of churches in local, regional, national, and international dialogues, whose mandates, although varied, all relate to promoting the unity of Christ's Church. It is virtually impossible to track all these dialogues, even on the international level, as the two volumes of *Growth in Agreement* indicate.[3] Activity of this kind and degree must be seen as *ecumen-*

1. See, e.g., Carl E. Braaten and Robert W. Jenson, eds., *In One Body Through the Cross: The Princeton Proposal for Christian Unity* (Grand Rapids, Mich.: Eerdmans, 2003).

2. For example, in August 2005 the General Council of Assemblies of God, a Pentecostal church generally negative toward the ecumenical movement, changed one of its by-laws that disapproved of ministers or churches participating in any ecumenical organizations so that it encouraged ministers or churches to fellowship with other Christians of "like precious faith." Bylaws, Article IX, Doctrines and Practices Disapproved, B. List of Doctrines and Practices Disapproved, Section 11.

3. Harding Meyer and Lukas Vischer, eds., *Growth in Agreement: Reports and Agreed Statements of Ecumenical Conversations on a World Level* (New York: Paulist, 1982); and Jeffrey Gros, Harding Meyer, and William G. Rusch, eds., *Growth in Agreement II: Reports and Agreed Statements of Ecumenical Conversations on a World Level, 1982-1998* (Grand Rapids, Mich.: Eerdmans, 1998).

ical reception on the part of churches that are willing to expend resources, talent, and energy to undertake it. Recent years have also shown an increasing number of churches to be not just open to such dialogue participation but also willing to give serious consideration to the conclusions of these dialogues and how they might affect the faith and life of the churches involved.[4]

In addition, a number of developments on national and international levels point to the emergence of *ecumenical reception*. For the most part, they consist of juridical actions that establish a new relationship between churches and often claim some level of agreement on theological issues that previously divided them. These juridical actions should not be considered *ecumenical reception* in and of themselves, but when they lead to implementation by way of membership in ecumenical organizations, changes in liturgies and theological education, and openness to cooperative work for social justice, we can discern preliminary *ecumenical reception* taking place.

It might seem that such efforts to implement juridical actions would be difficult to document, and so they are. Yet some national church bodies are endeavoring to be aware of them. It is commonly known, for example, that covenants exist between dioceses, synods, and congregations of Episcopal, Lutheran, and Roman Catholic churches in the United States, and that such groups have produced their own study materials to help deepen their mutual understanding and fellowship. A detailed map of this kind of preliminary *ecumenical reception* cannot be drawn at present, but it exists, and it requires further survey and study.

In the remainder of this chapter, the examples of *ecumenical reception* we will consider are largely based on juridical actions because they, and the events that follow in their wake, are much less difficult to document. As we turn to them, however, we should bear in mind that this

---

4. For example, see the *Charta Oecumenica* of the Roman Catholic Conference of Bishops in Europe and the Conference of European Churches. Although this text does not use the word *reception,* it is clear that the results of dialogue should be examined and whenever possible officially and in a binding manner be explained. *Charta Oecumenica,* §6, Dialoge fortsetzen (St. Gallen: Rat der Europäischen Bischofkonferenzen, 2001), p. 8.

other, less obvious, but no less significant *ecumenical reception* is taking place at the same time.

The Leuenberg Agreement

The Leuenberg Agreement is one example of *ecumenical reception* underway. With its origins in European conversations between Lutheran, Reformed, and United churches, the Leuenberg Agreement was submitted in 1971 to the European-Reformation churches. It was revised and completed at a further session at Leuenberg in 1973 and sent from there to the churches for approval by September 30, 1974.[5] It proposed church fellowship by way of concord, based on the consensus reached in an understanding of the gospel, so that churches with different confessional positions might accord one another fellowship in Word and sacrament. The agreement resulted in intense debates, but a number of churches declared their assent.

The 1973 conference included forty-five delegates from sixteen countries, most of whom were officially appointed church leaders; some were legal experts. Their final product was not lengthy; it contained a message to the participating churches, a presentation of the procedure and form for *reception,* the text of the actual agreement, and some comments on the declaration and realization of church fellowship based on a consensus reached in an understanding of the gospel so that churches with different confessional positions accord to each other fellowship in

---

5. "Agreement *(Konkordie)* among Reformation Churches in Europe," *Ecumenical Review* 25 (1973): 355-359; James E. Andrews and Joseph A. Burgess, eds., *An Invitation to Action: The Lutheran-Reformed Dialogue, Series III* (Philadelphia: Fortress, 1984), pp. 61-73. See also Elisabeth Schieffer, *Von Schauenburg nach Leuenberg: Entstehung und Bedeutung der Konkordie reformatorischer Kirchen in Europa* (Paderborn: Verlag Bonifatius, 1983); William G. Rusch and Daniel Martinsen, eds., *The Leuenberg Agreement and Lutheran-Reformed Relationships* (Minneapolis: Augsburg, 1989); and William G. Rusch, "Leuenberg Agreement," in *The Encyclopedia of Christianity,* vol. 3, ed. E. Fahlbusch, J. Milič Lochman, John Mbiti, Jaroslav Pelikan, and Lukas Vischer (Grand Rapids, Mich.: Eerdmans, 2003), pp. 245-47.

Word and sacrament. The exchange of this fellowship, rather than the exchange of voluminous texts, is at the heart of *ecumenical reception,* and the Leuenberg Agreement demonstrates this well.

Most European Lutheran and Reformed churches have signed the agreement, and in 1986 the United Evangelical Lutheran Church in Argentina became a signatory as well. In that same year, a study in Germany described the *ecumenical reception* of Leuenberg as a process involving pastors, parishes, and church leadership, all of whom were called upon to help determine whether the agreement reflected the faith of their churches.[6] Not surprisingly, there were some who did not believe their faith was reflected in it; in two notable cases, opposition centered on the understanding of biblical and confessional teachings, and in a third, the stalwart resistance of one bishop kept the process from going smoothly. All of this, of course, is part of the process.

The process of *ecumenical reception* inaugurated by the Leuenberg Agreement is still going on. The agreement itself calls for continuing theological conversation and study among the signing churches, which now include over 100 European churches of the Lutheran, Reformed, United, Methodist, Hussite, Waldensian, and Czech Brethren traditions and five South American Protestant churches. A series of studies undertaken by the Leuenberg churches has been published in English and German. A Leuenberg Fellowship has been established, which seeks to promote unity and community among the signing churches; it meets about every six years. Between assemblies, an executive committee led by a presidium of three persons oversees the ongoing work of the Fellowship.[7] The Leuenberg Agreement and the processes and organizations that have followed in its wake will no doubt continue to provide an important case study for *ecumenical reception* in the twenty-first century.

6. Hermann Brandt, ed., *Kirchliches Lehren in ökumenischer Verpflichtung: Eine Studie zur Rezeption ökumenischer Dokumente* (Stuttgart: Calwer, 1986).

7. See Rusch, "Leuenberg Agreement," in *The Encyclopedia of Christianity.*

A Covenant of Mission and Faith between the United Church of Christ in the United States and the Evangelical Church of the Union of the German Democratic Republic and the Federal Republic of Germany

These two churches, then in three different countries, enacted a resolution of a covenant of mission and faith in 1981. This juridical action, which certainly counts as an example of partial *ecumenical reception,* was based on some twenty-five years of visits and consultations, beginning in 1957 and continuing through the 1970s. In many ways these relations were based on a long history between the Evangelical and Reformed Church in the United States (one of the denominations that merged to form the United Church of Christ) and the Congregational Church in Germany. They were strengthened by joint work and support in the years immediately following World War II and by the ongoing work of the Faith and Order Commission of the World Council of Churches, especially by the actions of the New Delhi and Nairobi assemblies.

In 1976 a working group comprised of members of both the United Church of Christ and the Evangelical Church of the Union took up the question of the possibility of full communion between the two churches. A consultation was held in 1980. That same year the Synods of the Evangelical Church of the Union, East Region and West Region, voted for full church community with the United Church of Christ. In 1981 at its General Synod, the United Church of Christ approved the same action, establishing a covenant of mission and faith. As a result of this covenant a working group was put into place, cooperation has continued and been strengthened, and a number of consultations have occurred.

This covenant allows us to see the interplay of a number of factors that can hinder or help *ecumenical reception.* Clearly the two churches' concern about the unity and mission of the Church in the divided world is of paramount importance. But we can see a helping influence in the end of the Cold War, which allowed cooperation to proceed with fewer obstacles. Yet greater *ecumenical reception* may be hampered by the fact

that the churches are separated by geography and language. Nevertheless, this covenant must be noted as an example of churches in the ecumenical movement being willing to take steps together to receive the
fruits of dialogue and to express an even greater degree of unity.[8]

Baptism, Eucharist, and Ministry

We have already discussed *Baptism Eucharist and Ministry* at several
points in this book. But it is appropriate to mention it again here as an
example of preliminary *ecumenical reception.*

When it met in Lima, Peru, in January of 1982, the Commission on
Faith and Order put *Baptism, Eucharist and Ministry* into its final form
and initiated a process by which it would be sent to a large number of
churches for a response. In the years to come it would become evident
that the document occasioned an unprecedented interest in the modern
ecumenical movement.

Behind the decisions at Lima lay a long history of study and dialogue, reaching as far back as Lausanne in 1927, Edinburgh in 1937, Lund
in 1952, and Montreal in 1963. Of particular importance were meetings
that took place between those at Chichester in 1949 and Accra in 1974.
The Commission on Faith and Order issued significant documents on
baptism, Eucharist, and ministry throughout the 1960s and 1970s.[9] The
actual text of *Baptism, Eucharist and Ministry* was drafted from 1967
through 1972, beginning with the section on Eucharist and continuing
with baptism and ministry. From 1972 to 1974, several theologians discussed and refined the texts, and after the meeting of the Faith and Order Commission in Accra in 1974 these revised texts were sent to the
churches. Some 150 letters of response came back from various

8. A fuller description of the history behind the Covenant of Mission and Faith can
be found in Louis H. Gunnemann, *United and Uniting: The Meaning of an Ecclesial Journey*
(New York: United Church Press, 1987), pp. 59-84.

9. For a detailed account of this history, see William G. Rusch, "'Baptism, Eucharist
and Ministry' — and Reception," in *The Search for Visible Unity,* ed. Jeffrey Gros (New
York: Pilgrim, 1984), pp. 129-42.

churches, and in light of the concerns they raised, a small group of theologians from the Baptist, Lutheran, Methodist, Orthodox, Reformed, and Roman Catholic traditions gathered to work further on the texts. These efforts led to the final 1982 product.

Baptism, Eucharist and Ministry was not meant to be a complete dogmatic treatment of its three topics; it did not claim to resolve all differences on these topics. Rather, it was intended to be a theological contribution to the churches in the ecumenical movement, with churches absolutely free to identify with it, offer corrections to it, or reject it. The document itself claimed that a remarkable degree of convergence had been recognized and formulated, but it was up to the churches to make this final determination.[10]

The degree to which *Baptism, Eucharist and Ministry* was received can be measured in a number of ways. By the mid-1990s, the text had been translated into thirty-seven languages. Responses had come to Geneva from almost 200 churches, councils of churches, and individual theologians. Subsequent Faith and Order studies employed the document, and it became a resource in numerous bilateral dialogues on national and international levels, as well as in catechesis, theological education, and liturgical reform on local levels. Eventually, the Faith and Order Commission perceived that the response was large enough to require reports documenting it.[11]

The responses from the churches disclosed that further *ecumenical reception* requires additional work, particularly in the areas of the relationship between Scripture and tradition, the nature of the sacraments, and ecclesiology. Nevertheless, *Baptism, Eucharist and Ministry* stands as an example without parallel of preliminary or partial *reception.* It has received an extraordinary level of attention in churches, congregations,

---

10. For a summary of the entire process and history of *Baptism, Eucharist and Ministry* see Max Thurian, "*Baptism, Eucharist and Ministry* (the 'Lima text')" in *Dictionary of the Ecumenical Movement,* 2d ed., ed. N. Lossky, J. M. Bonino, J. Pobee, T. Stransky, G. Wainwright, and P. Webb (Geneva: World Council of Churches, 2000), pp. 90-93.

11. M. Thurian, ed., *Churches Respond to BEM,* Faith and Order Papers 129, 132, 135, 137, 143, 144 (Geneva: WCC, 1986-1988); and *Baptism, Eucharist and Ministry 1982-1990: Report on the Process and Responses,* Faith and Order Paper 149 (Geneva: WCC, 1991).

ecumenical organizations, theological faculties, and publications. More than half a million copies of the text have been published, giving it claim to be the most widely distributed and discussed text in the history of the ecumenical movement. Whether it will continue to play such a dominant role in the ecumenism of the twenty-first century remains to be seen, but as the twentieth century closed it was beyond dispute that it was an example of success in *ecumenical reception.*

The Meissen Agreement

Between 1985 and 1988 delegates from the Church of England, the Federation of the Evangelical Churches in the German Democratic Republic, and the Evangelical Church in Germany met to work out a basis for closer relations. The immediate cause for this dialogue was the 500th anniversary of the birth of Martin Luther, and the visit of Robert Runcie, the Archbishop of Canterbury, to the two Germanies to mark that occasion. Representatives from the churches met in London in 1987 to begin drafting a statement and completed their work the next year at Meissen in the German Democratic Republic. The document, known in English as the Meissen Agreement or the Meissen Declaration (and in German as *Die Meissener Erklärung*), consciously built on the work of earlier dialogues that had not yet been received by the churches. Containing six sections, it deals with the Church as a sign, instrument, and foretaste of the Kingdom of God; the Church as koinonia; growth toward full, visible unity; evidence of communion already shared; agreement in faith; and mutual acknowledgment and next steps.[12] The recognition of common faith, sacraments, and ministry in the text is impressive.

Yet the agreement neither allows for the exchangeability of ministers nor the participation of a bishop or priest of the Church of England in the laying-on-of hands at an ordination in the Evangelical Churches.

---

12. *The Meissen Agreement: Texts,* Occasional Paper 2 (London: The Council for Christian Unity of the General Synod of the Church of England, 1992).

From the Anglican perspective, sufficient consensus on the ordering of the Church was not reached. Nevertheless, in 1991 and 1992, the sponsoring churches of the dialogue leading up to the Meissen Agreement took official actions to approve the agreement and its implementation, with celebratory events taking place in London and Berlin in 1991.[13] The Meissen Agreement has two serious obstacles to move the involved churches from preliminary *reception* to fuller expressions of visible unity: the geographical separation of the churches, and the limits of the agreed theological consensus. These circumstances have not hindered the participating churches from forming partnerships with institutions of theological education, sharing libraries, holding joint official theological conferences, and exchanging church workers and ministers where desirable and possible in terms of the agreement.

The Porvoo Common Statement

Another example of churches entering into theological agreement and new relationship is the adoption of the Porvoo Common Statement by the British and Irish Anglican churches and the Lutheran churches of Estonia, Lithuania, Finland, Norway, and Sweden.[14] This adoption can be viewed as a preliminary expression of *ecumenical reception*. The churches that approved the Porvoo Common Statement have been regarded as entering into a fellowship, described as the Porvoo Communion, which is defined in the last chapter of the Common Statement in a text entitled "The Porvoo Declaration." The declaration is a short statement that the churches issued together in which they state they share one another's doctrinal basis and ordained ministries.

13. For the texts of the official actions by the various churches, see, Klaus Kremkau, ed., *Die Meissener Erklärung: Eine Dokumentation* (Hanover: Evangelische Kirche in Deutschland, 1993), pp. 142-244.

14. *Together in Mission and Ministry: The Porvoo Common Statement, with Essays on Church and Ministry in Northern Europe* (London: Church House Publishing, 1993); and O. Tjørhom, ed., *Apostolicity and Unity: Essays on the Porvoo Common Statement* (Grand Rapids, Mich.: Eerdmans, 2002).

Examples of Ecumenical Reception

The Porvoo Common Statement was put into its final form in Porvoo, Finland, in 1993 and sent to its sponsoring churches for action. The text was adopted by these churches at their various synods in 1994 and 1995. The adoption, however, was not unanimous. Although the Lutheran churches of Denmark and Latvia were part of the discussions, they did not approve the Porvoo Common Statement, and are thus at this point examples of non-*reception.*

As in the case with the Leuenberg Agreement, the history of the Porvoo Communion is rather lengthy, reaching back to conversations between the Church of England and the Church of Sweden in the late nineteenth and early twentieth centuries. In the 1920s and 1930s relationships of intercommunion were established between the Church of England and the Lutheran churches of Sweden, Finland, Estonia, and Latvia. In the 1950s intercommunion between the Church of England and the Lutheran churches of Norway, Denmark, and Iceland was approved, although from the Anglican perspective the theological and historical situation of these churches was different from that of Sweden, Finland, Estonia, and Latvia. All these agreements formed a background to the Porvoo Common Statement. Equally influential were such ecumenical texts as the Niagara Report of 1988, the Faith and Order text, *Baptism, Eucharist and Ministry,* and the Lutheran-Episcopal dialogue in the United States.[15]

For Anglicans, the chief reservation regarding communion with these Lutheran Nordic churches was the issue of the historic succession of bishops. The Lutheran concern, on the other hand, was one of theological confession. If church order was primary for Anglicans, theological clarity about justification, law and gospel, and the real presence in the Lord's Supper was foremost for Lutherans. The Porvoo Common Statement has chapters that address both sets of issues. Section 32 speaks of baptism, the Eucharist, and justification; sections 42, 44, and 50-54 take up the subject of church order. In these sections it is stated that episcopal succession does not alone guarantee the faithfulness of a

---

15. *The Niagara Report: Report of the Anglican-Lutheran Consultation on Episcope* (Cincinnati: Forward Movement Publications, 1988).

church to all the aspects of the apostolic faith. Yet Section 57 indicates that all the churches approving of the Porvoo Common Statement can affirm together the value and use of the sign of the historic episcopal succession.[16] As a result of the adoption of the Porvoo Common Statement, the signing Anglican churches have reinterpreted the past practices of these Lutheran churches as compatible with the Anglican insistence on succession; the signing Lutheran churches have committed themselves to a theology of episcopacy compatible with Anglicanism.

Since the early 1990s the member churches of the Porvoo communion have striven to implement the agreement. Clearly one of the significant challenges is geographical, since the churches do not overlap. Nevertheless, many contacts on the parish and diocesan levels have been established. Consultations have taken place between church leaders. A website has been put in place to share information about events and developments in the member churches. The Porvoo Common Statement has provided encouragement and sometimes a model for Anglican-Lutheran agreements in other parts of the world. The creation of an international Anglican-Lutheran Working Group is in part the result of the Porvoo Communion; it monitors and reports on Anglican-Lutheran developments to the Anglican Consultative Council and the Lutheran World Federation.

Future years will test the progress of *ecumenical reception* among the churches that have adopted the Porvoo Common Statement. The document has not been without its critics, who have raised questions about the lack of a complete ecclesiology in it. Especially in Germany, some Lutherans have wondered about the compatibility of the Leuenberg Agreement and the Porvoo Common Statement.[17] For such persons, a key

16. For a fuller description of the Porvoo Common Statement, see Risto Saarinen, "Porvoo Common Statement," in *The Encyclopedia of Christianity*, vol. 4, ed. E. Fahlbusch, J. Lochman, J. Mbiti, J. Pelikan, and L. Vischer (Grand Rapids, Mich.: Eerdmans, 2003), pp. 290-93.

17. See, for example, W. Hüffmeier and C. Podmore, eds., *Leuenberg, Meissen and Porvoo* (Frankfurt: Lembeck Verlag, 1996); and Risto Saarinen, "The Porvoo Common Statement and the Leuenberg Concord — Are They Compatible?" in *Apostolicity and Unity,* ed. Tjørhom.

question is whether the Porvoo Common Statement stresses too much external order at the expense of consensus on theological matters. These issues will continue to be discussed in the coming years, and the continued debate will affect the later stages of *ecumenical reception* of the Porvoo Communion, as too will signs of continued Lutheran willingness to order their churches' ministry in accord with the common statement.

Joint Declaration on the Doctrine of Justification

An example of *partial* or *preliminary reception* has also emerged from the Lutheran–Roman Catholic dialogue. This dialogue began on the international level as a result of the Second Vatican Council and issued its first report entitled *The Gospel and the Church*, but often known as the "Malta Report," in 1972. This dialogue text claimed that a far-reaching consensus was developing in the interpretation and understanding of the doctrine of justification. Yet the dialogue participants did not offer a detailed description of this consensus.[18] Some thirteen years later the Lutheran–Roman Catholic dialogue in the United States released a lengthy document with the title *Justification by Faith.* This national dialogue report claimed that a fundamental consensus on the gospel had been reached between Lutherans and Roman Catholics.[19] A third resource was a dialogue between the Roman Catholic Church in Germany and the Lutheran, Reformed, and United churches in Germany. The report of this dialogue, *Condemnations of the Reformation Era: Do They Still Divide?,* declared that the mutual condemnations of the sixteenth century in regard to justification do not apply to the present churches in a way that could divide them.[20]

18. *The Gospel and the Church* §26 in *Growth in Agreement: Reports and Statements of Ecumenical Agreement on a World Level,* ed. Jeffrey Gros and William G. Rusch (New York: Paulist, 1984), pp. 174-75.

19. H. George Anderson, T. Austin Murphy, and Joseph A. Burgess, eds., *Justification by Faith: Lutherans and Catholics in Dialogue VII* (Minneapolis: Augsburg, 1985), p. 74. The key paragraph is §164 of the declaration in the "Common Statement."

20. Karl Lehmann and Wolfhart Pannenberg, eds., *The Condemnations of the Reformation Era: Do They Still Divide?* (Minneapolis: Fortress, 1990), p. 68. See also

On the basis of these three resources, the Evangelical Lutheran Church in America requested the Lutheran World Federation to undertake a process in coordination with the Roman Catholic Church to consider declaring that the mutual condemnations on justification by Lutherans and Roman Catholics in the sixteenth century do not apply to the present ecumenical partnership. This process extended from 1993 until 1999, involving several drafts of a declaration-text and intense debate and criticism, especially by some German and American Lutheran theologians. Near the end of the process a response from the Roman Catholic Church raised questions for Lutherans as to whether there were differing interpretations of the *Joint Declaration*. This Lutheran concern led to the drafting of an "annex" to the *Joint Declaration*. The document faced far less criticism on the Roman Catholic side, but this may in part be explained by the fact that in the Catholic Church much less public debate was involved.[21]

On October 31, 1999, in Augsburg, Germany, an "Official Common Statement" affirming the *Joint Declaration on the Doctrine of Justification* in its entirety was signed by representatives of the Roman Catholic Church from the Vatican and the officers of the Lutheran World Federation on behalf of its member churches. By this act of signing, the *Joint Declaration* became an official statement of the member churches of the Lutheran World Federation and the Roman Catholic Church. The affirmed consensus was no longer only the opinion of dialogue participants but of churches, who were declaring that a consensus existed between them on the basic truths of the doctrine of justification and that

---

K. Lehmann, M. Root, and W. G. Rusch, eds., *Justification by Faith: Do the Sixteenth Century Condemnations Still Apply?* (New York: Continuum, 1997).

21. For one view of the entire process leading to the *Joint Declaration on Justification*, see William G. Rusch, "The History and Methodology of the *Joint Declaration on Justification:* A Case Study in Ecumenical Reception," in *Agapè: Études en l'honneur de Mgr Pierre Duprey,* ed. Jean-Marie Tillard (Geneva: Centre Orthodoxe du Patriarcat Oecuménique, 2000), pp. 169-84. See also Michael Root, "Joint Declaration on the Doctrine of Justification," in *The Encyclopedia of Christianity,* vol. 3, ed. Fahlbusch et al., pp. 72-74; and Matthias Turk, "The Reception of the Joint Declaration on the Doctrine of Justification," *One in Christ* 37/2 (2002): 61-66.

therefore the mutual condemnations of the sixteenth century on this topic appear in a new light.[22]

The *Joint Declaration* itself is not a lengthy document. After a short introduction, it contains five major sections divided into 44 numbered paragraphs. The first section presents the biblical basis for the agreement; the second describes how justification is an ecumenical issue. The third and fourth sections form the core of the document, setting forth a common understanding of justification and applying it to a number of traditionally divisive subjects for Lutherans and Roman Catholics. The last section states the importance of the *Joint Declaration* and the need for the agreement to influence the life and teachings of both the Lutheran churches and the Roman Catholic Church. Thus the *Joint Declaration* itself acknowledges that it is an example of preliminary *reception* even on this one admittedly critical doctrine for Lutheran–Roman Catholic relations. At the time of the signing, Pope John Paul II and others spoke of the *Joint Declaration* as a milestone on the journey toward full unity between Lutherans and Roman Catholics.

Interest has been expressed in enlarging the number of churches that could agree with the consensus contained in the *Joint Declaration,* and to this end a conference was held at Yale University in 2000.[23] The following year a consultation was organized by the Lutheran World Federation and the Pontifical Council for Promoting Christian Unity of the Vatican on the same theme.[24]

One result of such efforts was the approval by the World Methodist Council, meeting in Seoul in 2006, of an agreement that expressed a concurrence with the consensus of the *Joint Declaration.*[25] The Method-

22. *Joint Declaration on the Doctrine of Justification* (Grand Rapids, Mich.: Eerdmans Publishing Company, 2000), §41.

23. William G. Rusch, ed., *Justification and the Future of the Ecumenical Movement: The Joint Declaration on the Doctrine of Justification* (Collegeville, Minn.: Liturgical Press, 2003).

24. See *Unity in Faith: The Joint Declaration on the Doctrine of Justification in a Wider Ecumenical Context* (Vatican City: Pontifical Council for Promoting Christian Unity; and Geneva: The Lutheran World Federation, 2002).

25. On the action of the World Methodist Conference, see Kenneth Loyer, "Prog-

ist Council signed a declaration affirming the statements Lutherans and Roman Catholics made together and indicates Methodist agreement with the consensus reached by the Lutherans and the Catholics.[26] Thus without signing the *Joint Declaration* itself — which would have been impossible for Methodists since they did not participate in the condemnations of the Reformation era — the World Methodist Council agreed with the differentiated consensus expressed in the *Joint Declaration*.

As with other examples of partial *reception* portrayed in this chapter, only the future will tell whether this significant example of preliminary *reception* by Lutherans and Roman Catholics will lead to a fuller agreement on justification and other topics that in the past and present have visibly divided Lutheran and Roman Catholic churches. The years immediately after the Augsburg signing have not been particularly encouraging; the full import of the *Joint Declaration* seems lost on many. Some observers have pointed out tendencies to pull back from the agreement and a hesitation to explore its fuller implications for the churches. If this perception is accurate, it shows the continuing difficulties for churches to arrive at *ecumenical reception*.

Anglican–Roman Catholic International Commission

Before turning our attention to the ecumenical scene in the United States, it will be insightful to comment on one other international dialogue. This bilateral conversation has not been described in the preceding list because it has not resulted in any official juridical action by both sponsoring churches. Nevertheless, the efforts of the Anglican–Roman

---

ress and Possibility: Ecumenism at the 2006 World Methodist Conference," *Ecumenical Trends* 35/9 (October 2006): 9-14; and Theodor Dieter, "Methodists Declare Agreement with Joint Declaration," *Newsletter of the Institute for Ecumenical Research Strasbourg* 9 (Winter 2006/07): 2-3.

26. The text is entitled *Methodist Statement of Association with the Joint Declaration on the Doctrine of Justification.* Available online at www.worldmethodistcouncil.org/filesworld_methodist_council_and_the_jddj.pdf.

Catholic International Commission (ARCIC) should be mentioned in any list of *ecumenical reception.*

The Commission began its work in the context of the events and developments of the Second Vatican Council. A preliminary commission met in 1967-68 and issued the Malta Report, the mandate for which was given in 1966 in the *Common Declaration* of Pope Paul VI and the Archbishop of Canterbury, Michael Ramsey. It was to engage in a serious dialogue based on the gospels and the ancient common tradition, which would lead to the unity in truth for which Christ prayed. This mandate led to two series of dialogues that by 2004 had resulted in ten agreed statements. The first series published statements and elucidations on Eucharistic doctrine, ministry and ordination, and authority. The second series issued statements on justification, ecclesiology, morals, authority, and Mary. The first series claimed to have reached substantial agreement on the topics it addressed; the second series concluded that its work on authority showed sufficient agreement on universal primacy that such a primacy could be shared before the churches arrived at full communion.[27]

None of these statements received official approval by the two churches.[28] The Lambeth Conference of 1988 did, however, officially receive the work of the first series of dialogues. Yet such action does not bind individual Anglican churches. In 1991, the Vatican's Congregation for the Doctrine of the Faith replied to the agreed statements on ministry and ordination. Most readers saw this response as negative and re-

27. For the background of the Anglican–Roman Catholic International Commission and its work, see "Anglican–Roman Catholic Dialogue," in *Dictionary of the Ecumenical Movement,* 2d rev. ed., pp. 33-35; Meyer and Vischer, eds., *Growth in Agreement,* pp. 61-129; and Jeffrey Gros, Harding Meyer, and William G. Rusch, eds., *Growth in Agreement II: Reports and Agreed Statements of Ecumenical Conversations on a World Level, 1984-1998* (Grand Rapids, Mich.: Eerdmans Publishing Company, 2000), pp. 312-72; *The Gift of Authority: Authority in the Church III* (New York: Church Publishing, 1999); and *Mary: Grace and Hope in Christ* (Harrisburg, Pa.: Morehouse Publishing, 2005). See also Angelo Maffeis, *Ecumenical Dialogue* (Collegeville, Minn.: Liturgical Press, 2005), p. 43.

28. This statement is certainly true on the international level. It is also true that the Episcopal Church in the United States as one Anglican Church in its General Convention in 1985 received the agreed statements on Eucharist and ministry.

quiring identical common formulations of these topics. The same concern had been raised by the same Congregation in 1986 about the document on ecclesiology. Later the Vatican, in response to certain "clarification" from the dialogue participants, apparently agreed with the statements on the Eucharist and ministry. In 1994, Cardinal Edward I. Cassidy, as the President of the Pontifical Council for Promoting Christian Unity, indicated that no further work needed to be done on the Eucharist, but the question of who was to preside at the Eucharist was unsolved. There has been no response to the statements of the second series of the dialogue.

This brief overview demonstrates once again the difficulties that confront the *ecumenical reception* of the work of any dialogue. What is notable is not the lack of *ecumenical reception* but the amount of it that has been possible in a relatively short time, given its many challenges.

Examples from the Ecumenical Movement in the United States

The instances of *partial* or *preliminary ecumenical reception* given to this point have been international and predominantly European in scope. An analysis of examples of preliminary *ecumenical reception* on a global basis is not possible in the present context. However, an illustrative (but not exhaustive) survey of American developments is appropriate, given both the expected primary readership of this work and the number of available examples in the United States.[29]

---

29. Mention should be made that evidence of *ecumenical reception* is not lacking in Canada. The first major union of churches in the modern ecumenical movement was the United Church of Canada in 1925. In 2001 the Anglican Church of Canada and the Evangelical Lutheran in Canada adopted a revised version of *Called to Full Communion: The Waterloo Declaration*. See Thomas Best, "United and Uniting Churches," in *Dictionary of the Ecumenical Movement*, pp. 1164-68; Richard G. Leggett, ed., *A Companion to the Waterloo Declaration: Commentary and Essays on Lutheran-Anglican Relations in Canada* (Toronto: Anglican Book Centre, 1999); and the online text of the document, available at http://anglican.ca/ministry/inchurch/waterloo_revised_annotated.html.

Examples of Ecumenical Reception

The Consultation on Church Union

A multilateral instance of efforts for *ecumenical reception* is the Consultation on Church Union, which can trace its origins back to a sermon delivered by Eugene Carson Blake in 1960 in San Francisco. The Consultation itself began to function in 1962. By 1970 its membership included nine United States churches and its designated purpose was to explore the establishment of a church that was truly catholic, truly evangelical, and truly reformed. During the early years of the Consultation effort was expended to reach theological agreement on such issues as ministry and sacraments among the nine churches. By 1970, after two years of intensive work, a Plan of Union was drafted that called for institutional merger of the member churches in the Consultation. The year 1970 also saw the churches reach an agreement on the recognition of baptism. The study program for the Plan of Union revealed that by the early 1970s the model of institutional merger was not acceptable. This conclusion led in 1979 to a model of unity based on the idea of the churches covenanting together, a model deeply influenced by the notion of conciliar fellowship defined at the Nairobi Assembly of the World Council of Churches. The suggestion of covenanting had as its purpose to allow for organic unity and considerable diversity without an organizational merger. In 1984 a "COCU Consensus" was published.

The nine churches in the Consultation in 1989 declared this consensus an expression of the apostolic faith, order, worship, and witness of the Church. This was preceded in 1988 with a document, "The Churches in Covenant Communion," which was approved by seven of the nine denominations. This plan for the formation of a covenant relationship was not approved by presbyteries of the Presbyterian Church (U.S.A.) or by the Episcopal Church. In both cases approval was withheld over issues regarding ordained ministry.

In 1999 a new step was taken by the member churches of the Consultation. A new relation was proposed to be called Churches Uniting in Christ. This new relationship came into being in 2002 and was inaugurated and celebrated liturgically in the Week of Prayer for Christian Unity of that year. The characteristics of Churches Uniting In Christ included mutual recognition of the churches involved as authentic expressions of churches of Jesus Christ, mutual recognition of baptism, mutual recognition of the Apostles' and Nicene Creeds, a commitment to common mission and to common celebration of the Lord's Supper, and finally a common commitment to combat racism. This relationship had nine constituent church bodies: the African Methodist Episcopal Church, the African Methodist Episcopal Zion Church, the Christian Church (Disciples of Christ), the Christian Methodist Episcopal Church, the Episcopal Church in the USA, the International Council of Community Churches, the Presbyterian Church (U.S.A.), the United Church of Christ, and the United Methodist Church. By 2002 the Evangelical Lutheran Church in America and the Moravian Church (Northern Province) related to Churches Uniting in Christ as "Partners in Mission and Dialogue." Conspicuously, the question of ministry was left open to ongoing dialogue, and the pursuit of consensus on that topic has continued since 2002.[30]

The Consultation on Church Union, now in its new formulation as Churches Uniting in Christ, is an example of a degree of *ecumenical reception* on the part of the nine member-churches and to a lesser degree the two "partners in mission and dialogue." The history and present state of involvement of this group have brought churches together which were previously isolated from each other. They have gained greater knowledge and appreciation of each other and their histories. There have been sharing and *reception* in areas of liturgy, education, and social justice. No doubt these churches have changed in this process. The original vision of unity has been given up and replaced with another model. The history of the Consultation, and now Churches Uniting, indicates how difficult *ecumenical reception* is. Whether the present theological work will lead these churches out of their impasse on ministry is not something we can predict.

30. For a brief history of the Consultation on Church Union and bibliography, see Gerald F. Moede and Michael Kinnamon, "Consultation on Church Union," in *Dictionary of the Ecumenical Movement*, pp. 252-53.

The United Church of Christ and the Christian Church (Disciples of Christ)

In 1985 the United Church of Christ and the Christian Church (Disciples of Christ) in the United States entered into an ecumenical partnership, which may be considered an example of partial *ecumenical reception*. Both church bodies kept their identity, but together they entered into a relationship that included a commitment to Christian unity and the mutual recognition of members; mutual recognition and reconciliation of ministers; the commitment to common service and decision-making; and a confession of sin. These churches saw this action as part of the larger commitment to the Consultation on Church Union to which they both belonged. Three marks of this relationship were common mission, joint theological work, and common worship. A partnership committee was established with members of both churches and some other churches in the Consultation on Church Union to implement work in these areas. This relationship was put in place by the approval of a document entitled *Declaration of Ecumenical Partnership* by the General Synod of the United Church of Christ and the General Assembly of the Christian Church (Disciples of Christ).[31] This text outlines the nature of the partnership, but it says little about the theological consensus that makes the partnership possible. The underlying assumption seems to be that there is a fundamental theological agreement between both of these churches.

Lutheran-Reformed Relations

The Evangelical Lutheran Church in America, the Presbyterian Church (U.S.A.), the Reformed Church in America, and the United Church of

---

31. The text of the *Declaration of Ecumenical Partnership* may be found in Louis H. Gunnemann, *United and Uniting: The Meaning of an Ecclesial Journey* (New York: United Church Press, 1987), pp. 181-85. The same volume gives a description of the early history of the partnership on pp. 85-109.

Christ adopted a document entitled "Formula of Agreement" in 1997 to enter into a process to bring them into a relationship of full communion.[32] This juridical action should be considered an example of preliminary *reception*. Behind this decision stood years of dialogue in the United States, as well as some controversy.

The first Lutheran-Reformed dialogue in the United States began in 1962 and published its report, *Marburg Revisited,* in 1966.[33] Although this dialogue text concluded that there were no insuperable obstacles to pulpit and altar fellowship, no action leading to such a relation was taken by any of the constituent churches. A second round of Lutheran-Reformed dialogue was at work between 1972 and 1974. Hampered by the internal disputes within the Lutheran Church–Missouri Synod, this dialogue issued a brief report and encouraged further Lutheran-Reformed dialogue.

The third round of Lutheran-Reformed dialogue met from 1981 until 1983, when it issued its report, *An Invitation to Action,* which built both on the Leuenberg Agreement and *Marburg Revisited.*[34] This 1983 text contained statements on justification, the Lord's Supper, and ministry. It strongly encouraged its sponsoring churches to establish altar and pulpit fellowship and to inaugurate a process of *ecumenical reception.* The reactions to this report showed that the Lutheran churches involved were not all at the same place. The former American Lutheran Church and the Association of Evangelical Lutheran Churches, along with the Presbyterian Church (U.S.A.) and the Reformed Church in America, adopted the recommendations of the report. The Lutheran Church in America did not adopt the report, out of concern regarding whether sufficient agreement had been reached on the Lord's Supper

32. "A Formula of Agreement between the Evangelical Lutheran Church in America, the Presbyterian Church (U.S.A.), the Reformed Church in America and the United Church of Christ on entering into full communion on the basis of *A Common Calling*" (Chicago: The Evangelical Lutheran Church in America, n.d.).

33. Paul C. Empie and James I. McCord, eds., *Marburg Revisited* (Minneapolis: Augsburg, 1966).

34. James E. Andrews and Joseph A. Burgess, eds., *An Invitation to Action: Lutheran-Reformed Dialogue, Series III, 1981-1983* (Philadelphia: Fortress, 1984).

and ministry, but it requested the matter be referred to the soon-to-exist Evangelical Lutheran Church in America.

Thus in 1988 the Evangelical Lutheran Church in America and the three Reformed churches — the Presbyterian Church (U.S.A.), the Reformed Church in America, and the United Church of Christ (a member of the dialogue from the time of *Marburg Revisited*) — entered into theological conversations.[35] The term "conversations" was deliberately selected to avoid prejudging whether further dialogue was required. These conversations released their report in 1992, entitling it *A Common Calling: the Witness of Our Reformation Churches in North America Today.*[36] This report called for all the participating churches to enter into full communion with each other, recognizing each other's members and ministers (with the possibility of exchangeability) and each other's baptism and Lord's Supper; lifting any condemnations; and engaging in common mission.[37] These recommendations were incorporated into the document *Formula of Agreement* and approved in 1997 by all concerned. Since that date the Evangelical Lutheran Church in Americ, the Presbyterian Church (U.S.A.), the Reformed Church in America, and the United Church of Christ have been in a process of partial *ecumenical reception,* which will lead, they trust, to full-fledged *ecumenical reception.* The ecumenical will for such a relationship is being, and will be, tested in the twenty-first century as these churches face internal tensions that could threaten their unity and their willingness to be ecumenically open.[38]

---

35. See William G. Rusch and Daniel F. Martenson, eds., *The Leuenberg Agreement and Lutheran-Reformed Relationships* (Minneapolis: Augsburg Publishing House, 1989).

36. Keith Nickle and Timothy Lull, eds., *A Common Calling: The Witness of Our Reformation Churches in North America Today* (Minneapolis: Augsburg Publishing House, 1993).

37. See *The Orderly Exchange of Ordained Ministers of Word and Sacrament: Principles, Policies, and Procedures — Churches Participating in A Formula of Agreement* (Louisville: Office of the General Assembly Presbyterian Church [U.S.A.], 2000).

38. For an overview of the Lutheran-Reformed dialogue, see Paul R. Fries, "Lutheran-Reformed Dialogue" in *Dictionary of the Ecumenical Movement,* pp. 718-20.

Episcopal-Lutheran Relations

In the United States sustained dialogue between Episcopalians and Lutherans began after an invitation was offered by the General Convention of the Episcopal Church in 1967. The first sessions of dialogue took place in 1969, with the goal of exploring the possibilities and problems for a more extended dialogue to deal with fellowship and unity. Participants included the Episcopal Church, the American Lutheran Church, the Lutheran Church in America, and the Lutheran Church–Missouri Synod. The dialogue, later referred to as Lutheran-Episcopal Dialogue I (LED I), issued its report in 1973. Although this first series of dialogue proposed to the sponsoring churches that they authorize intercommunion, the churches took no action.[39] A second series of dialogue was approved, which worked from 1976 to 1980. It published its report in the following year.[40] This text contained joint statements on justification, the gospel, Eucharistic presence, and the authority of Scripture. It asked the churches to recognize each other as churches, work out a policy of interim Eucharistic hospitality, and authorize a third series of dialogues on the topic of ministry. The Lutheran Church–Missouri Synod, however, did not endorse these recommendations.

Nevertheless, these proposals in a modified form were taken up and approved by the three Lutheran churches that in 1988 would join to form the Evangelical Lutheran Church in America, and by the Episcopal Church. This modified form of recommendations, known as the Lutheran-Episcopal Agreement of 1982, provided that these churches recognize each other as churches in which the gospel is preached, encourage common mission, establish an interim sharing of the Eucharist, and authorize a third series of dialogues to explore the implications of the gospel and address the question of ministry in the Church.[41] The third series commenced its work in the following year,

39. *Lutheran-Episcopal Dialogue: A Progress Report* (Cincinnati: Forward Movement Publications, 1973).

40. *Lutheran-Episcopal Dialogue: The Report of the Lutheran-Episcopal Dialogue: Second Series 1976-1980* (Cincinnati: Forward Movement Publications, 1981).

41. See, for example, *The Lutheran-Episcopal Agreement: Commentary and Guide-*

and met until 1993. It divided its assignment into two parts. Thus in 1988 it issued the report *Implications of the Gospel* and in 1991 *"Towards Full Communion" and "Concordat of Agreement."*[42] A majority of the dialogue participants saw these two texts as the fulfillment of the dialogue's mandate and as the rationale for the Episcopal Church in the USA and the Evangelical Lutheran Church in America to take juridical actions that would lead them to a relationship of full communion.

Especially after the publication of the last dialogue report, *"Towards Full Communion" and "Concordat of Agreement,"* an intense debate broke out in the Evangelical Lutheran Church in America about the compatibility of the dialogue's proposals about ministry with the Lutheran confessional understanding of that topic. This dispute illustrates how difficult *ecumenical reception* can be, especially when it is perceived as threatening confessional identity — regardless of whether such a perception is accurate. In 1997 the General Convention of the Episcopal Church in both its houses approved *Concordat of Agreement;* the Evangelical Lutheran Church in America in the same year at its churchwide assembly narrowly failed to secure the two-thirds vote required for adoption.

This defeat caused a new series of conversations between the two churches, which resulted in 1999 with a revision of the original *Concordat of Agreement* now entitled *Called to Common Mission.*[43] Its approval by both churches led to its provisions coming into effect in January of 2001, and was marked by a liturgical celebration. The entire history of

---

lines (New York: Division for World Mission and Ecumenism, Lutheran Church in America, 1983).

42. William A. Norgren and William G. Rusch, eds., *Implications of the Gospel: Lutheran-Episcopal Dialogue, Series III* (Minneapolis: Augsburg Fortress, 1988) and William A. Norgren and William G. Rusch, eds., *"Towards Full Communion" and "Concordat of Agreement," Lutheran-Episcopal Dialogue, Series III* (Minneapolis: Augsburg Fortress, 1991). See also James E. Griffiss and Daniel F. Martensen, eds., *A Commentary on "Concordat of Agreement"* (Minneapolis: Augsburg Fortress, 1994) and Daniel F. Martensen, ed., *Concordat of Agreement: Supporting Essays* (Minneapolis: Augsburg Fortress, 1995).

43. *Called to Common Mission: A Lutheran Proposal for a Revision of the Concordat of Agreement* (Chicago: Evangelical Lutheran Church in America, 1998).

the Lutheran-Episcopal dialogue in the United States offers a clear picture of the difficulty of the success of even partial *ecumenical reception* after a sustained dialogue between two churches with many similarities and ample interpretative materials supplied to those churches.[44]

This fact is further underscored by a unilateral action taken by the Evangelical Lutheran Church in America after the inauguration of *Called to Common Mission* in January of 2001. Later in the same year at its churchwide assembly, the Evangelical Lutheran Church in America amended a bylaw to grant exceptions under certain circumstances to a key provision of *Call to Common Mission* regarding the ordination of ministers. From the perspective of ecumenical theology, this action is an obvious case of non-*reception* of an ecumenical agreement, to be regretted for its content and its methodology. It will make future progress of moving from preliminary *ecumenical reception* to fuller expressions of *ecumenical reception* more difficult.[45]

Lutheran-Moravian Relations

Another national dialogue that offers an example of preliminary *ecumenical reception* is that between the Evangelical Lutheran Church in America and the Moravian Church in America (the Northern and Southern Provinces). These churches in the 1990s entered in a theological dialogue, which issued a report entitled *Following Our Shepherd to Full Communion*.[46] This report proposed a relationship of full communion on the basis of a common understanding of the Word of God as described in Scripture. The proposal of full communion was approved by the two provinces of the Moravian Church in 1998 and by the Evangelical Lutheran Church in America in 1999. Both juridical

---

44. For a brief history of Episcopal-Lutheran dialogue, see David Tustin, "Anglican-Lutheran Dialogue," in *Dictionary of the Ecumenical Movement*, pp. 24-26.

45. See Chapter 5, footnote 29.

46. *Following Our Shepherd to Full Communion: Report of the Lutheran-Moravian Dialogue with Recommendations for Full Communion in Worship, Fellowship and Mission* (Chicago: Evangelical Lutheran Church in America, 1998).

actions should be seen as examples of preliminary *ecumenical reception*. Lutherans and Moravians declared that they confess a common faith and share the sacraments. They made commitments to evangelism, witness, and service together, as well to the exchange of ordained ministers when necessary for the mission of the Church.[47] Like other instances of partial *reception* noted in this chapter, the future will disclose to what degree these initial actions are able to lead to fuller *ecumenical reception* between Lutherans and Moravians in the United States.

Conclusions

The examples reviewed in this chapter provide certain insights into the theme of this volume. They show, first of all, that in virtually every case it is not possible to speak of *ecumenical reception* as a static goal that has been reached by even a few divided churches. *Ecumenical reception,* as all these chapters have endeavored to stress, is part of an ongoing and dynamic process. At best, indications can be given to certain juridical actions by churches that can be taken as signs of preliminary or partial *ecumenical reception.* In most of these cases the final determination as to whether or not these initial changes called forth by these juridical actions will permanently affect the relationship of the divided churches in question is unknown. In some of these instances, there is evidence soon after the juridical action that hesitations about continuing down the road of *ecumenical reception* have appeared. This seems to be the case with the *Joint Declaration on the Doctrine of Justification* on the Lutheran side. It is also true with the relationship established by *Called to Common Mission* in the United States between Episcopalians and Lutherans. The same phenomenon can be noted by the churches involved in the multilateral Churches Uniting in Christ. All of these hesitations and

---

47. *Principles for the Orderly Exchange of Ordained Ministers of Word and Sacrament; Evangelical Lutheran Church in America–Moravian Church in America, Northern and Southern Provinces* (Chicago: Evangelical Lutheran Church in America, 2001).

others that could be mentioned reveal the fragile nature of the degree of *ecumenical reception* attained to date.

In this regard all the churches struggling to receive the results of the ecumenical movement are in largely uncharted territory and facing questions that they have not been required to confront before. In many cases the core of their identity is being examined. It should be noted that to date there is virtually no evidence of even partial or preliminary *ecumenical reception* of ethical and gender issues that are now showing the potential of being church-dividing within and among churches. Until some clarity is obtained on these subjects, further steps toward *ecumenical reception* will be hampered.[48]

What is clear in the above account is that without the Holy Spirit churches will easily lose their way in the journey toward receiving gifts from each other. While the function of the place of the Spirit in this process can never be forgotten or ignored, there are two concepts emerging in ecumenical theology that may indeed be gifts of the Spirit to assist the churches in *ecumenical reception*. These concepts are the subject of the next chapter.

48. On this topic see Ellen K. Wondra, "We Ordain Them, They Don't," in *One Lord, One Faith, One Baptism: Studies in Christian Ecclesiality and Ecumenism in Honor of J. Robert Wright,* ed. Marsha L. Dutton and Patrick Terrell Gray (Grand Rapids, Mich.: Eerdmans Publishing Company, 2006), pp. 219-40.

Chapter 7

Resources for *Ecumenical Reception*

O ur study of *reception* to this point has described a phenomenon in the life and thought of the Church across centuries. The characteristics of the most recent form of *reception,* which we have called *ecumenical reception,* have been observed, as have the difficulties, challenges, and gifts of *ecumenical reception* — even in its most preliminary stages.

As the twenty-first century opens, there is ample evidence that the modern ecumenical movement is in danger of losing its focus on the visible unity of Christ's Church. The more that genuine *ecumenical reception* can take place among the divided churches, the more that the ecumenical movement can regain its proper *raison d'être.* The preceding chapters have sufficiently illustrated the formidable obstacles to this type of *reception.* The topic of this chapter is to examine two concepts, or resources, that have emerged within ecumenical theology which may assist in rendering *ecumenical reception* less arduous for churches in the ecumenical movement.

Both concepts have, interestingly enough, arisen within the ecumenical movement itself rather than being imposed externally. They both address two key hindrances in advance toward the visible unity of Christ's Church: the difficulty, if not impossibility, of arriving at *total* agreement among divided churches on doctrinal matters; and the equally difficult task of identifying or constructing common structures for churches to live out their visible unity.

Differentiated Consensus

It became apparent early in the ecumenical enterprise that at least two approaches to securing doctrinal consensus among divided churches would not succeed. The first scenario would be that church A would convince church B that church A's position was correct and the position of church B was in error. The result would be that church B would convert to the position of church A. Both theologically and politically, the likelihood of such a converting action is remote at best, and indeed a survey of the many bilateral dialogues yields little or no evidence of this occurring.

The other approach would entail that two churches in doctrinal disagreement on a specific topic would attempt to move out of their disagreement by merging their different doctrines into a new synthesis. Here again is an approach marked by extreme difficulties, if not impossibilities, and there is no evidence that it ever was successful in any meaningful way.

The abundance of dialogue reports on the national, regional, and international levels provides ample data for a detailed study of how these dialogues, independently in most cases, have created a specific methodology and moved away from one particular understanding of unity for the ecumenical movement — that is, the idea that to be unified, churches would have to surrender their unique identities. In the initial decades of the ecumenical movement there was a presupposition, an assumed opinion, that the visible unity of divided churches would come when organic union took place among divided churches. For this organic union to occur confessional identities would have to be surrendered. Anglicans, Lutherans, and Reformed, for example, would cease to exist as Anglicans, Lutherans, and Reformed. This model was favored in the early years of the work of the Commission on Faith and Order and considerably influenced by the participation of Anglicans during those years.[1]

This situation changed dramatically when the Roman Catholic Church as a result of the Second Vatican Council became a participant in the ecumenical movement. While this church certainly did not oppose the multilateral work of Faith and Order, and quickly became a full member of the Faith and Order Commission, there was a strong Roman Catholic preference for bilateral dialogues. It is not mere chance that the years immediately after Vatican II saw a proliferation of such dialogues. This approach was in harmony with the Roman Catholic Church's self-understanding, which did not allow for the loss of confessional identity. The result of this Roman Catholic involvement was a new understanding of the goal of the ecumenical movement that no longer contained a contradiction between confessional identity and ecumenism itself.

This understanding is expressed in an obvious way in the *Decree on Ecumenism* of the Second Vatican Council where the aim of the ecumenical movement is described as arriving at consensus.[2] Theological understanding and a visible unity could exist among churches that were organizationally separate. Thus a fundamental assumption arose that the dialogues even with their specific goals, which could differ, shared a commitment to seek a theological consensus that made visible unity possible. A new ecumenical methodology, avoiding both conversion and synthesis, was emerging that saw consensus as the presupposition and enabling resource for the unity of the Church.[3]

1. For a fuller discussion of this whole issue, see Harding Meyer, *That All May Be One: Perceptions and Models of Ecumenicity* (Grand Rapids, Mich.: Eerdmans Publishing Company, 1999), pp. 79-100.

2. See especially *Decree on Ecumenism,* pp. 2-4.

3. See William G. Rusch, "Structures of Unity: The Next Ecumenical Challenge — A Possible Way Forward," *Ecclesiology* 2:1 (September 2005): 107-22 and in *Ecumenical Trends* 34:9 (October 2005): 2-8; and Harding Meyer, "Ecumenical Consensus: Our Quest for and the Emerging Structures of Consensus," *Gregorianum* 77:2 (1996): 213-225. Fundamental for this discussion is the critical article by Harding Meyer, "Die Prägung einer Formel: Ursprung und Intention" in *Einheit — Aber Wie?: Zur Tragfähigkeit der ökumenischen Formel vom "differenzierten Konsens,"* in *Quaestiones Disputatae* 184, ed. Harald Wagner (Freiburg: Herder Verlag, 2000), pp. 36-58.

Initially, this methodology, which appeared gradually, was unnamed. It had a key characteristic in that it affirmed unity and diversity as the twofold aim of the dialogues, and thus of the ecumenical movement itself. This affirmation was present regardless of whether the exact expression "unity and diversity" was present in dialogue reports.[4] What was extremely critical and influential in this methodology was the insistence that confessional identity was not to be given up. On the contrary, it was to be positively acknowledged and celebrated. This approach forced the dialogue participants to develop and promote a view of the unity of the Church as a unity or koinonia, a fellowship of churches of varying confessional identities living, practicing, and showing forth full visible unity.[5]

In recent years this gradually developing and recognized methodology has been termed "differentiated consensus" or, in German, "differenziter Konsens." The German is significant because most of the earlier identification and discussion of the concept was conducted in German. Harding Meyer of the Lutheran World Federation-related Institute for Ecumenical Research at Strasbourg has been a major figure in the identification of the concept and the application of the specific German phrase to describe it.[6]

Whether in its German original or its English translation, the expression is apt and accurate. It highlights two critical aspects of the concept and methodology. Differentiated consensus is characterized by a double structure that is intentional and apparent. This trait has been pictured in terms of two levels: there is a first or fundamental level, and this is a level of consensus. On this level the agreement is real and essential. It is neither a general, loose agreement nor a compromise. Yet this agreement or consensus of the first level exists along with a second level

---

4. This point is documented in Günther Gassmann and Harding Meyer, *The Unity of the Church: Requirements and Structures,* Lutheran Federation Report 15 (Geneva: Lutheran World Federation, 1983).

5. See Meyer, "Die Prägung einer Formel: Ursprung und Intention," p. 36.

6. One of the most significant articles on this topic, as indicated in footnote 2, is Meyer's "Die Prägung einer Formel: Ursprung und Intention," which unfortunately has not been translated into English.

where there are remaining differences, and these differences are as real and essential as the agreements of the first level. Differentiated consensus allows for unity of faith through, not despite, different formulas to express that faith.

The key factor is a characteristic that all these differences share: they do not challenge the consensus or agreement on the first level. In other words, these continuing and relevant differences are evaluated as tolerable or bearable in regard to the consensus on the first level. Such a schema allows for unity and diversity. It, in fact, not only allows a place for difference in itself, but it integrates such differences within a unity.[7] The differences are not something strange to this consensus. They are integral to it. The result of this fact is that differentiated consensus will always include these two levels or two different sets of statements. One set articulates the agreement identified on an issue that has been in dispute. This agreement in content is foundational and critical in terms of what it contains. The second set of statements discloses in what ways and for what reasons these remaining differences can be considered as admissible and thus not calling into question the agreement.

This methodology can be observed in several of the texts we considered in Chapter 6. It is not merely accidental that these documents which were the basis for juridical action leading to preliminary *ecumenical reception* are evidence for differentiated consensus.

A good illustration of the use of differentiated consensus in an ecumenical text that led to a juridical action changing the relations among churches is the Leuenberg Agreement originally involving Lutheran, Reformed, and United churches in Germany. A careful examination of this document discloses a methodology that starts with a declared recognition of common elements in the churches of the Reformation; continues by noting changed elements in the contemporary situation; and moves to an articulation of a discovered consensus in the gospel, which includes justification, preaching, baptism, the Lord's Supper, and Christology. Within these aspects of the gospel it is acknowledged that differences remain between the Lutheran and Reformed traditions. The

7. See Rusch, "Structures of Unity."

conclusions drawn are that the consensus on these various issues means that the condemnations of the Reformation confessions in respect of the Lord's Supper, Christology, and predestination are inapplicable.

Thus they are no longer an obstacle to church fellowship, although the point is affirmed that the condemnations pronounced by the Reformers are not irrelevant. The Leuenberg Agreement never employs the terminology of differentiated consensus. Yet it is clear that its methodology is that of fundamental consensus with differences not challenging that consensus. Here are exactly the characteristics that describe differentiated consensus. This differentiated consensus allows for a declaration of fellowship and a realization of this fellowship.[8]

A second example of a similar phenomenon is the Porvoo Common Statement. This text, as was noted in the previous chapter, provided the basis for juridical action establishing a new relation between the Anglican churches of Britain and Ireland and the Nordic and Baltic Lutheran churches.

An investigation of the text of the Porvoo Common Statement discloses a number of important points. The first section emphasizes the common characteristics these churches share in their faith and understanding of mission. Like the Leuenberg Agreement, the Porvoo Statement acknowledges the contemporary situation of Europe.[9] The next part of the text moves on to describe the nature and the unity of the Church, emphasizing the freshness of the contemporary situation and the views held jointly by Anglicans and Lutherans. In this account of consensus diversity is not only recognized, but it is affirmed because of its richness.[10] The agreement in faith is the topic of the third section. The nature of this agreement is substantial, reflecting a high degree of consensus. Nevertheless, this agreement is carefully nuanced in the entire document, and a recurring theme in the Porvoo Statement is that

8. See the Leuenberg Agreement, especially sections 1 through 3, in James E. Andrews and Joseph A. Burgess, eds., *An Invitation to Action: The Lutheran-Reformed Dialogue, Series III* (Philadelphia: Fortress, 1984), pp. 66-70.

9. *Together in Mission and Ministry: The Porvoo Statement with Essays on Church and Ministry in Northern Europe* (London: Church of England, 1993), pp. 7-9.

10. *Together in Mission and Ministry*, pp. 10-15.

this remaining difference is such that the claimed consensus is not to-tal.[11] This motif of substantial agreement and legitimate difference is also to be found in the fourth part of the statement, which takes up epis-copacy and apostolicity.[12]

The entire text is disclosing an approach on two levels: a level of fundamental agreement and a second level of continuing differences that does not impair the agreement on the first level — a methodology, in other words, of differentiated consensus. The Porvoo Statement ar-gues that there is a far-reaching, but not total, consensus between Angli-cans and Lutherans on such matters as faith, mission, and ministry. It is this differentiated consensus that allows a new stage of the journey to-gether in faith, but without a denial by Anglicans or Lutherans of a par-ticularity within their own churches, e.g., the specific Anglican and Lu-theran perspectives on historic episcopal succession. Here again is another example of differentiated consensus as a methodology provid-ing the rationale for steps that must be viewed as signs of preliminary or partial *ecumenical reception.*

Yet another example of an ecumenical text exhibiting differentiated consensus is the *Joint Declaration on the Doctrine of Justification* — in-deed, few ecumenical texts are as transparent in their use of differenti-ated consensus as this one. In paragraph 40, the churches of the Lu-theran World Federation and the Roman Catholic Church state together that a consensus in the basic truths of the doctrine of justifica-tion exists between Lutherans and Roman Catholics.[13] This consensus makes possible two statements in paragraph 41: first, that the teachings of the Lutheran churches presented in the Declaration do not fall under the condemnations of the Council of Trent; and second, that the con-demnations in the Lutheran Confessions do not apply to the teaching of the Roman Catholic Church presented in this Declaration.[14]

These conclusions are possible because in paragraph 15 a central

11. *Together in Mission and Ministry,* pp. 16, 21.

12. *Together in Mission and Ministry,* pp. 22-29.

13. *Joint Declaration on the Doctrine of Justification* (Grand Rapids: Mich.: Eerdmans Publishing Company, 2000), pp. 25-26.

14. *Joint Declaration on the Doctrine of Justification,* p. 26.

statement of the document is given, that is, "By grace alone, in faith in Christ's saving work and not because of any merit on our part, we are accepted by God and receive the Holy Spirit, who renews our hearts while equipping and calling us to good works."[15] Here the Declaration is expressing a fundamental agreement or consensus. Catholics and Lutherans are agreeing that God alone is the ultimate ground and goal of human hope. God has shown faithfulness over and against human unfaithfulness once and for all in Jesus Christ without human merit and involvement.

However, in this context of consensus, there is recognition and even appreciation of the remaining differences between Lutherans and Roman Catholics. Seven further agreements are noted as explications of the fundamental consensus expressed in paragraph 15. In these seven agreements what is sought is neither a common language nor common formulation. Rather, what is explored is the question of whether these traditionally church-dividing statements continue to have any church-dividing results or whether they can be understood and interpreted as differing explanations of the fundamental agreement. In this regard the conclusion of the Declaration is that these differences do not endanger the fundamental consensus. This is true in regard to human powerlessness and sin in paragraph 19, justification as the forgiveness of sins and making righteous in paragraph 22, justification by faith and through grace in paragraph 25, the justified as sinner in paragraph 28, law and gospel in paragraph 31, assurance of salvation in paragraph 34, and the good works of the justified in paragraph 37.[16]

This repeating pattern in the *Joint Declaration on the Doctrine of Justification* is a clear example of the use of the methodology of the concept of differentiated consensus. The bipolar pattern of two levels, one of fundamental agreement on a specific topic and a second of differences which do not challenge the fundamental agreement, is the methodology of differentiated consensus and it is clearly employed in the *Joint Declaration on the Doctrine of Justification*. The establishment of a new rela-

15. *Joint Declaration on the Doctrine of Justification,* p. 15.
16. See *Joint Declaration on the Doctrine of Justification,* pp. 17, 18, 19, 20, 22, 23, and 24.

tion between the member churches of the Lutheran World Federation and the Roman Catholic Church is rooted in a document that calls for ecumenical advance precisely on the basis of differentiated consensus.

The three documents reviewed here offer sufficient proof of the importance of differentiated consensus for the future of the ecumenical movement. There is little doubt that differentiated consensus will be employed in the coming years as a way to overcome the past divisions of churches. The usefulness and validity of the methodology will rest on the answer to one question: Is the claimed fundamental consensus of the first level able to function in such a manner that the different explications on the second level do not call into question or endanger this basic consensus? If the response to this question can be positive, the positions of various traditions or churches are liberated from having to reach a consensus in formulation and language on every possible church-dividing question. It should not be minimized, of course, that this approach challenges the self-understanding of many traditions and churches.

In regard to this situation a number of relevant items should be mentioned. First, the signing and putting into practice of both the Leuenberg Agreement in 1973 and of the *Joint Declaration on the Doctrine of Justification* in 1999 moved differentiated consensus out of the realm of theory and into the area of practice and acceptance. Differentiated consensus has already provided for varying degrees of *ecumenical reception.*

Second, while in the history of Christian thought a variety of languages and differences of theological elaboration and emphases have been suspected of concealing ambiguities, if not church-dividing differences, there is also evidence in the Christian tradition of the use and appreciation of the diversity of the expression of the faith. The New Testament contains four gospels, and in its other books reflects a rich diversity.[17] The Church of the early centuries was not monolithic. Local churches remained in communion while celebrating Easter on different days. The schools of Antioch and Alexandria remained in fellowship

17. See James D. G. Dunn, *Unity and Diversity in the New Testament: An Inquiry into the Character of Earliest Christianity* (Philadelphia: Westminster, 1977).

over the years despite their tensions. In the medieval period Dun Scotus and later the Council of Florence could accept different expressions about the procession of the Holy Spirit.[18] In the sixteenth century the Augsburg Confession in its oft-cited article 7 expressed the possibility of living with difference.[19] The same thought is also to be found in the preface to the same Confession, in articles 15 and 28.[20] All these instances reveal that prior to the modern era some precedents for differentiated consensus can be found.

In more recent times, additional forerunners of differentiated consensus can be pointed out. Pope John XXIII's opening speech, *Gaudet Mater Ecclesia,* at the Second Vatican Council made the critical distinction between the "deposit of the faith that is the truths contained in our venerable doctrine" and "the form in which these truths are declared." The pope insists that different forms are able to conserve the same meaning and content.[21] This distinction was repeated in the *Decree on Ecumenism* itself of the Council.[22]

The discussions about basic consensus (Grundkonsensus) in the late 1970s and early 1980s may also be viewed as preliminary to the development of the concept and methodology of differentiated consensus. In these explorations a main concern was the issue could one identify among the various expressions of the Christian faith and different traditions or churches a "basis consensus." The debate centered particularly around some type of ecumenical recognition of the Augsburg Confession in 1980 and the Nicene-Constantinopolitan Creed in 1981.[23]

18. See Duns Scotus, *I Sent.,* d. XI, q. 1; and Joseph Gill, "Constance et Bâsle" in *Histoire des conciles oecuménique,* vol. 9 (Paris: l'Orante, 1965), esp. pp. 246-49.

19. Robert Kolb and Timothy J. Wengert, eds., *The Book of Concord: The Confessions of the Evangelical Lutheran Church* (Minneapolis: Fortress, 2000), pp. 42-43.

20. *Book of Concord,* pp. 30-35, 48-49, and 90-103.

21. See Walter M. Abbott, S.J., ed., *The Documents of Vatican II* (New York: Crossroad, 1989), pp. 710-19, esp. 715; and Giuseppe Alberigo and Joseph A. Komonchak, eds., *History of Vatican II,* Vol. II (Maryknoll, N.Y.: Orbis, 1997), pp. 14-19.

22. *Decree on Ecumenism,* 4.

23. See Harding Meyer, "Die Prägung einer Formel: Ursprung und Intention," pp. 50-54; A. Birmelé and H. Meyer, eds., *Grundkonsens-Grunddifferenz* (Frankfurt: Lembeck and Bonifatius, 1992); Joseph A. Burgess, ed., *The Role of the Augsburg Confes-*

In 1986 Joseph Ratzinger, now Pope Benedict XVI, who had done much to raise the question of "recognition" of the Augsburg Confession, published an article arguing for the legitimacy and even the desirability of a pluralistic understanding of truth as based on a correct understanding of the nature of theology. Ratzinger makes the point that Christian truth must be viewed not as a monotony but as a symphony where the multiplicity of historical expressions of faith are acknowledged as an organic characteristic of Christian truth, which surpasses human measurement.[24]

Pope John Paul II in 1995 issued his encyclical letter, *Ut unum sint,* on commitment to ecumenism. In this encyclical the pope repeats and thus endorses the statement of Pope John XXIII on the distinction between the deposit of the faith and the formulation in which it is expressed.[25] Later in the same text John Paul II states the need in ecumenical progress for mutual enrichment among the divided churches. He is indicating that the particular doctrinal stress of other churches can be regarded as a source of richness for the Roman Catholic Church itself.[26] This is an idea which was expressed earlier at the Second Vatican Council in the *Decree on Ecumenism,* especially in §3 and 4, as noted above. The pontiff lifts up in his encyclical as a specific example of this the agreements reached between the Roman Catholic Church and Eastern Orthodox Churches.[27] It is certainly appropriate to see in the text of this encyclical an implicit, if not explicit, approval for what is being termed differentiated consensus.

What is alluded to in *Ut unum sint* can be observed in two ecumenical agreements entered into by the Roman Catholic Church with ancient Orthodox churches which do not share the same number of sacra-

---

sion: *Catholic and Lutheran Views* (Philadelphia: Fortress, 1980); George Wolfgang Forell and James F. McCue, eds., *Confessing One Faith: A Joint Commentary on the Augsburg Confession by Lutheran and Catholic Theologians* (Minneapolis: Augsburg, 1982); and Joseph A. Burgess, ed., *In Search of Christian Unity: Basic Consensus/Basic Differences* (Minneapolis: Fortress, 1991).

24. Joseph Ratzinger, "Pluralismus als Frage an Kirche und Theologie," *Forum Katholische Theologie* 2 (1986): 81-96.

25. *Ut unum sint* (Vatican City: Libreria Editrice Vaticana, 1995), §81

26. *Ut unum sint,* §87.

27. *Ut unum sint,* §50-58, see also §19.

ments or the same canon of Holy Scripture.[28] Such agreements are not only examples of preliminary *ecumenical reception* but also of the acceptance of differentiated consensus.

Theodore Dieter of the Lutheran World Federation-related Institute for Ecumenical Research in Strasbourg, France has forcefully made the point that differentiated consensus should no longer be regarded as a theory. He makes the case that there is now sufficient evidence of its ecumenical acceptance. He has specifically indicated that the full implications of this decision for the Roman Catholic Church are still to be seen.[29] This insight is, no doubt, for all the churches in the ecumenical movement an accurate evaluation.

All of this is not to say that differentiated consensus is a panacea that will provide for unlimited ecumenical advance. Although there are precedents in church history and in modern ecumenical texts for differentiated consensus, it will strike many as a novelty with overtones of compromise. It will also appear heavily academic, Lutheran, and German. Most of the discussion of the concept has been in German by Lutheran theologians, and many of these books and articles remain untranslated. The *reception* of differentiated consensus itself will be difficult even among church leaders, ecumenists, and theologians.

An example of the discussion about differentiated consensus that is just beginning is an important article by Annemarie C. Mayer of the Catholic-Theological Faculty at the Institute for Ecumenical Research at University of Tübingen.[30] The nationality and location of the author should be noted. Mayer believes that differentiated consensus has be-

28. This statement is certainly accurate in terms of the agreement between the Roman Catholic Church and the Assyrian Orthodox Church of the East. For a selection of relevant texts, see Jeffrey Gros, Harding Meyer, and William G. Rusch, eds., *Growth in Agreement II: Reports and Agreed Statements of Ecumenical Conversations on a World Level, 1984-1998* (Grand Rapids, Mich.: Eerdmans Publishing Company, 2000), pp. 688-712.

29. Theodore Dieter, "Die Folgen der Gemeiner Erklärung zur Recht aus evangelischer Sicht," *Una Sancta* 59:2 (2004): 134-144.

30. Annemarie C. Mayer, "Language Serving Unity? Linguistic-Hermeneutical Considerations of a Basic Ecumenical Problem," *Pro Ecclesia*, Vol. XV, No. 2 (Spring 2006): 205-222.

come the present-day golden rule of ecumenical hermeneutics. This is probably a statement that only a German could make at this time! She grants that differentiated consensus has as its goal a unity in diversity and that it achieves this purpose by stressing an underlying unity in denominationally different churches. Mayer continues that it is exactly for this reason that differentiated consensus has its limitations and is thus open to criticism. She states that the inner dynamic toward greater unity, which would bear a more effective witness to the one God, is lost by this idea. Differentiated consensus, according to Mayer, aims too low. She also believes that differentiated consensus leads to the perpetuation of a multi-denominational reality.

Such comments at least raise the question of whether the true nature of the concept of differentiated consensus has been grasped here. The unity achieved in differentiated consensus is neither some lower type of unity nor a provisional state of unity. It is a real unity in a tension with a real diversity, which the concept argues has been the nature of Christian unity throughout the centuries of Christianity.

Mayer also critiques differentiated consensus from a linguistic point of view and concludes that it places heavy burdens on those who employ it by its use of technical terminology and controversial theology. These problems can lead to identifying all differences to misunderstanding or attributing all the misunderstandings to the interlocutor and assuming that one's own church has properly understood the matter. Mayer concludes that if this happens differentiated consensus has become a two-edged sword. It can enable ecumenical processes, but it can also cast doubt on them.

After an analysis of the present situation of dialogue under the headings of "the horror of 'equalizing' and assimilation," "the phantom of identical understanding," and "antagonism between truth and pluralism," Mayer proposes an improvement for differentiated consensus on the basis of the semiotic theory of Umberto Eco, described as "relative nonambiguity." This theory and the use of metaphors can result in a modified and nuanced model of differentiated consensus. This model, according to Mayer, leads to unity in diversity because it allows space for nonindifferent understanding.

The purpose of the inclusion of an account of Mayer's article here is not to critique her suggestions. It is rather to offer one example of the ongoing discussion of differentiated consensus, which will no doubt continue and expand in the coming years. Clearly a question lurking here is whether the unity of differentiated consensus is true unity.

Another instance of the continuing influence of differentiated consensus comes from the 2006 assembly of the Community of Protestant Churches in Europe — the Leuenberg Fellowship. The final report of this assembly, held in Budapest in September of 2006, entitled *Freedom is Binding,* deals with continuing dialogues in Europe. The specific model stressed and endorsed is the model of the Leuenberg Agreement, i.e., the model of unity and diversity with an ecumenical consensus achieved on the basis of differentiated consensus. In view of the rationale of the Leuenberg Fellowship, such a position is not surprising, but it is also additional evidence of the continuing application of differentiated consensus.[31]

Differentiated Participation

Even the proponents of this concept acknowledge that in itself differentiated consensus will not lead the churches to full visible unity. This evaluation is accurate because the concept does not and cannot address one essential element of visible unity — that of structures. A visibly united Church of Christ will need to be structured. The question of structures has indeed a theological dimension. For example, questions about the episcopal office or about the papacy are not issues of structure alone but also of theology. In regard to this theological dimension differentiated consensus can be anticipated to be of assistance.

31. See *Freedom is Binding,* §3 and also §4, where *ecumenical reception* is encouraged. Available online at http://www.leuenberg.net. See also Elisabeth Parmentier, "Freedom is Binding," *Newsletter of the Institute for Ecumenical Research, Strasbourg,* Issue 9 (Winter 2006/07): 1-2, where it is stated, "The general assembly declared the model of differentiated consensus to be appropriate not only for inner-Protestant relations, but also a promising model for dialogue with other churches."

Yet when the conversation moves to the topic of the ecclesial and institutional forms of agreed structures for visible unity, differentiated consensus on theological matters does not eliminate the remaining barriers on the way to that unity. The question becomes: is there an additional concept that would address this structural issue?

In endeavoring to answer this question, again Harding Meyer supplies a possible way forward.[32] For this concept I am indebted to him, as I have acknowledged in several publications.[33] We both have been thinking independently about a concept or methodology to supplement differentiated consensus, but it is Meyer whose clarity of thought and suggestion of a specific term has been critical.

As the title of the article by Meyer indicates, his particular concern here is how there could be a sharing by Protestant, or non-episcopal, churches in the historic office of bishop. The initial sections of the article describe the nature of dialogue, the concept of consensus, and the character of ecumenical consensus as a differentiated consensus. Meyer explains how through differentiated consensus a level of theological understanding can be developed about the office of bishop. This theological understanding can lead to the realization of equivalent aspects of a non-episcopal and episcopal office of oversight in the churches. Such a realization could in turn result in a mutual recognition of the offices of church leadership. Yet as Meyer forcefully points out, such recognition is not a mutual participation in the office of bishop or church-leadership.[34] Thus it is only a limited, preliminary *ecumenical reception.*

As a means of continuing ecumenical initiative, Meyer suggests a new term and idea in ecumenical theology: "differentiated participation." The expression and the methodology it contains have parallels with differentiated consensus. It is clear that before differentiated par-

32. Harding Meyer, "Evangelische Teilhabe am Episkopat?" *Stimmen der Zeit* 4 (2005): 244-256, which appears in English translation with the title "Differentiated Participation: The Possibility of Protestant Sharing in the Historic Office of Bishop," *Ecumenical Trends* 34:9 (2005): 9-15.

33. See for example, William G. Rusch, "Structures of Unity," esp. footnote 39.

34. Harding Meyer, "Differentiated Participation," p. 11.

ticipation could be evoked there must be a differentiated consensus on a topic with structural dimensions. If a differentiated consensus has been identified, then differentiated participation may be applied. By means of differentiated participation, divided churches could in common participate in a structure, or office of the Church, e.g., the historic office of bishop, with diverse interpretation, accentuation, and assessments of this office.[35] There would be a level of agreement about what participation in such a specific office or structure would mean, then there would be a second level of differences about this participation, which do not call into question the first level of agreement.

I have argued that such an idea has already been placed into ecumenical practice in the United States in the agreement between the Episcopal Church and the Evangelical Lutheran Church in America, wherein both churches have agreed to participate together in the historic office of bishop with a differentiated consensus about this office, a mutual recognition of each other's office of oversight, and a differentiated participation in a common office of oversight.[36]

Whether the methodology of differentiated participation could be applied to the papacy by a non–Roman Catholic church is a more complex question. I examined this possibility in regard to Lutheran–Roman Catholic relations.[37] In this article, I sought to show that there is a tradition within Lutheran confessional theology that would allow for a differentiated consensus on the papal office. This differentiated consensus finds support in the teaching of Philip Melanchthon in his *De potestate et primatu papae,* which is one of the documents of the Lutheran Confessions. In this treatise Melanchthon makes the case that the Lutheran Reformation's insistence on the *ius humanum* nature of the papal office is basically and intentionally not a categorical denial of its possible *ius divinum* nature.[38]

35. Meyer, "Differentiated Participation," 13.

36. This position is expounded in greater detail in William G. Rusch, "Structures of Unity."

37. William G. Rusch, "A Contemporary Lutheran View of the Papacy: The Possibility for Ecumenical Advance," *Centro Pro Unione Bulletin* 70 (Fall 2006): 19-24.

38. Rusch, "A Contemporary Lutheran View of the Papacy," p. 20.

If this basis does exist and there is already an acknowledged differentiated consensus on the doctrine of justification by grace through faith, I argued that Lutherans could entertain a differentiated participation in the papacy as an office of unity within the Church and as an office exercising a primacy with the Church. I noted in conclusion that differentiated consensus *and* differentiated participation as components for a contemporary Lutheran view of the papacy would require further exploration.[39]

A final answer to this question of a Lutheran differentiated participation in the papacy lies obviously in a more distant future, but in view of the Lutheran Confessional teachings, recent developments in Roman Catholic theology, and conclusions of Lutheran–Roman Catholic dialogue, it should not be dismissed out of hand. In any case the testing of such possibilities will continue the evaluation of both differentiated consensus and differentiated participation as paths leading beyond the present ecumenical impasse in so many areas.

Conclusions

This chapter offers an overview of two concepts or methodologies that have evolved in the course of ecumenical dialogue and thinking since the rise of the modern ecumenical movement in the early twentieth century. The argument can be made that both differentiated consensus and differentiated participation are more than ecumenical theories or wishful thinking on the part of die-hard ecumenists. There is evidence that at least at the dialogue level both concepts have been employed, both in dialogue conclusions and to some measure in official actions of *ecumenical reception* by some churches. Both concepts thus can promote *ecumenical reception,* but both concepts themselves must be *received* by the churches and not just by individual participants in the dialogues. In this regard, it must be acknowledged that the churches in the ecumenical movement are only in the initial stages of the process. Both differenti-

39. Rusch, "A Contemporary Lutheran View of the Papacy," pp. 23-24.

ated consensus and differentiated participation are little-known and open to misunderstanding. This statement is probably truer of the latter concept than the former. Yet some of the reactions to the *Joint Declaration on the Doctrine of Justification* reveal that such an evaluation of the situation with differentiated consensus is correct.[40] Differentiated participation is less tested in the ecumenical area and less certain in the process of *ecumenical reception* by the churches.

The future of *ecumenical reception* in the churches in the twenty-first century will depend in many ways on the success of the *reception* of differentiated consensus and differentiated participation as viable approaches to overcome historical church-dividing issues of doctrine and structure. At this time it is premature to draw any final conclusions. There are indeed signs of positive evaluation and acceptance of these methodologies in certain churches. But in the same churches there is evidence of the resistance to these methodologies and outright rejection. It is difficult to see even for those committed to ecumenical progress by way of theological consensus where simply more theological dialogue between divided churches without the acceptance of tools to receive the work and conclusions of these dialogues will lead to ecumenical advance in the near future.

To conclude this volume, we will now attempt to summarize the content of the previous chapters and draw some tentative conclusions regarding *ecumenical reception.*

---

40. See for example, Dietz Lange, ed., *Überholte Verurteilungen? Die Gegensätze in der Lehre von Rechtfertigung, Abendmahl und Amt zwischen dem Konzil von Trient und der Reformation — damals und heute* (Göttingen: Vandenhoeck & Ruprecht, 1991), esp. pp. 28-88.

Chapter 8

Conclusions

I f the narrative of the preceding pages has had any cogency, it will
appear immediately that a final chapter of "conclusions" is both in-
appropriate and impossible. *Reception,* and this includes *ecumenical
reception,* is a lively, ongoing process in the life of the Church. As
long as the Church of Christ continues its journey in time and space,
an ultimate word cannot be written about *reception.* One of the purposes of the present work has been to make that point evident. Yet it
should be acceptable to pause at this time in the history of the Church
and of the ecumenical movement to determine what recent reflections about, and actions of, *reception* can remind us about its challenge and opportunity for the faith and followers of Christ in the
twenty-first century.

We began by observing that *reception* is an extensive and rich term
that has more than just theological dimensions. This larger context of
reception can be a resource for its theological investigation. The greater
scene was noted, but it was clearly stated that the precise focus of this
work was the *theological* setting and understanding of *reception.*

In the process of investigating *reception,* it was observed that after
long periods of neglect in the past century the centrality of *reception* for
the Christian faith was appreciated once again. *Reception* plays a key
role in the biblical text; it is the process by which God's revelation is

135

handed on ("traditioned") to each new generation in the history of Israel and of the Church.

Still, for all its significance *reception* is not open to easy definition. Everyone knows what *reception* is until someone is called upon to furnish a short and specific definition. In its most elemental form, theological *reception* must involve the receiving of something not previously available to a people, a community, or an individual. In the revelation of the Triune God, a community through history received God's Word, God's promises, and in a finality God's incarnate Son, Jesus Christ. This *reception* was available in a preeminent way in Scripture, was handed down in the Tradition of the Church, and was given expression in liturgy, in conciliar decisions, and in the life of the Christian communities. Such *reception* was never only doctrinal or juridical. In the early centuries of the Church *reception* functioned easily among the local churches, although it would be misleading to paint an idealized picture of it even in the early centuries of Christianity. After bitter doctrinal disputes beginning in the fourth century, divided local churches received less and less from each other. For the Western church, by the Middle Ages *reception* was perceived, if at all, within the narrow confines of councils and canon law, virtually forgotten outside the realms of canon law and some patristic studies.

The twentieth century witnessed the rediscovery of *reception* in theology. The catalysts for this new discovery were the modern ecumenical movement and the Second Vatican Council. The urgent challenge of how divided churches were to receive from each other and receive the modern ecumenical movement and its fruits brought *reception* back to center stage. But this was no longer the *reception* of the undivided Church. A new form of *reception* was demanded, and so we have drawn the distinction between *classical reception* and *ecumenical reception*. The major stress of this book has been on the latter expression of *reception*.

A new setting and purpose for this *reception* arose with the rise of the modern ecumenical movement at the beginning of the twentieth century. Earlier *classical reception* was regarded as a phenomenon of an undivided church, where local churches received from each other liturgical practices, local customs, and theological insights. The usual, but not only, locus for this *reception* was churches gathered into councils.

Ecumenical reception could not take place in such a conciliar setting, for it was impossible for doctrinally divided churches to enter into a true council together. Indeed, one of the goals of *ecumenical reception* was to allow the type of theological consensus to occur that would make a truly ecumenical council again possible in the history of the Church. In view of this situation the similarities and differences between both kinds of *reception* were described.

The present account has presented argument that *ecumenical reception* is not simply a dream or hope of those committed to the visible unity of the Church. In spite of all the challenges, if not outright obstacles at times, there is a record that *ecumenical reception* in a preliminary or partial form has occurred on a number of occasions. Such *preliminary ecumenical reception* has usually taken place in the form of juridical actions. These juridical decisions were not self-standing. Behind them stood texts with an understandable language and theology for all concerned, personal and trusting contacts among key persons, and a demonstrable practical benefit from adoption. By such actions, the sponsoring churches agreed to the conclusions of the dialogue at least to the degree that recognition of some consensus took place on a previously disputed point of doctrine and often the relationship between the divided churches was changed.

These steps are the initial stages of a probably long and unfolding process leading the churches closer to full unity. Thus there is the dynamic nature of *ecumenical reception*. But these first actions should not be minimized, for they represent decisions that at one time had been perceived as impossible. They demonstrate that *ecumenical reception* is a reality.

In view of this fact, it is necessary to examine what concepts or methodologies have allowed these instances of *ecumenical reception* to occur. With an acknowledged indebtedness to German ecumenical scholarship, this volume has proposed that two concepts have enabled *ecumenical reception* to happen and that these concepts hold the promise for further steps in the process of *ecumenical reception*. These concepts and the methodologies they embody have fairly recently become known as differentiated consensus and differentiated participation. Both ideas arose out of the dialogical process itself. They were not something conceived before the start of the dialogues. Both are rooted in and function on the basis that the unity of Christ's Church has not been, and will not be in the future, a unity that is uniformity. Rather this unity has been, and will be, a unity in diversity.

This volume holds to the premise that the future success of the ecumenical movement will largely rest on the acceptance or rejection of these two concepts. If theological consensus and common participation in some form of commonly visible structures are requirements for genuine ecumenical advance beyond mere cooperation, then the potential and possibility of differentiated consensus and differentiated participation cannot be ignored.

The ecumenical testing of both methodologies is in an initial phase. The willingness of some dialogues and their sponsoring churches to pursue them is encouraging. Yet voices of caution or even rejection can be heard, and only time and experience will tell whether differentiated consensus and differentiated participation will take hold in the churches.

Within recent years it has become almost commonplace to speak of the crisis in the ecumenical movement, or of the fact that the ecumenical movement has lost its way and its proper focus. There is much evidence to document such contentions.[1] A sense of ecumenical urgency has declined. Churches are willing to live in visible disunity and often are not scandalized by this situation. Cooperation seems a satisfactory substitute for visible unity. The goal of the ecumenical movement is unfocused. The solid results of many of the bilateral dialogues are ignored

---

1. See for example, Harding Meyer, *That All May Be One: Perceptions and Models of Ecumenicity* (Grand Rapids, Mich.: Eerdmans Publishing Company, 1999), esp. pp. 151-56; William G. Rusch, "An Ecumenist Looks at Two Centuries," *Ecumenical Trends* 31:6 (2002): 1-7; and "What is Keeping the Churches Apart?" *Ecumenical Trends* 32:1 (2003): 1-4; and Carl E. Braaten and Robert W. Jenson, eds., *In One Body Through the Cross: The Princeton Proposal for Christian Unity* (Grand Rapids, Mich.: Eerdmans Publishing Company, 2003).

or resisted. As this work has demonstrated, *reception* of the dialogues has proven much more difficult than once would have been imagined. Councils of churches as vehicles for the ecumenical movement have in many cases become ineffective. They have surrendered the goal of visible unity as a primary concern, and often been transformed into cooperative agencies for interfaith corporation. This is not to say that interfaith is an unimportant area of work; rather, it is to say that there is a distinction required between ecumenical work and interfaith work. It is precisely in this context of ecumenical decline and uncertainty that *ecumenical reception* may hold the key to ecumenical recovery and renewal.

Ecumenical reception, made possible by differentiated consensus and differentiated participation, may offer the deeply divided and indifferent-to-their-scandal churches the gift to recover under the guidance of the Spirit their journey to that goal which is clearly the will of their Lord. The challenge and the opportunity of *ecumenical reception* may well shape the story of the Church in the twenty-first century in ways yet to be imagined. Thus there certainly cannot now be either a final word on or a conclusion to the venture of *ecumenical reception.*

Index